Fouga Magister
An Irish Perspective

By Joe Maxwell and Radu Brînzan

The opinions expressed in this book are those of the authors and do not necessarily reflect those of the Irish Air Corps or the Department of Defence.

ISBN 978-0-9562624-1-7
Book Design and layout: Declan Maxwell
Graphic Illustrations: Radu Brînzan

This book is typeset in Bembo 9.7 pt.
Printed by W&G Baird, Caulside Drive, Antrim, Northern Ireland.

First published by Max Decals Publications Ltd. August 2012.
© Joe Maxwell and Radu Brînzan
www.maxdecals.com

maxdecals.com

About the authors: Joe Maxwell produces the Max Decals range of model aircraft accessories. He co-authored the Irish Air Corps – An Illustrated Guide with Patrick J. Cummins in 2009 and continues to write occasional articles for magazines. Radu Brinzan produces the RB Productions range of model aircraft accessories and tools. His previous book The I.A.R. 80 & I.A.R. 81 Airframe, Systems & Equipment was published in 2011.

Front and rear cover photos: These shots were taken by Commandant Dave Corcoran on the last occasion on which five Irish Air Corps Fouga Magisters flew together in September 1996. These photos were taken on a Minolta 700SI SLR with Sigma 18-35mm Lens. The lens was fitted with a polarizing filter and spot metered on the fuselage of the Fouga. The camera was in shutter priority mode with a speed of at least 1/350 of a second. The film used was colour slide.

Contents

Acknowledgements

The authors could not have brought this book to fruition without the support and assistance of a great many people. We would like to thank Brigadier General Paul Fry, General Officer Commanding Irish Air Corps for his support for this project. He also clarified a great many details regarding the replacement of the Fouga by the PC-9 and provided us with some photos from his own collection. The liaison officer for this project was Lieutenant Colonel Kevin Byrne. Kevin's contribution and enthusiasm has been immense. He has cheerfully answered all our questions and provided us with helpful advice. Thanks also to Captain Brendan O'Dowd. We would like to thank the recently retired Commandant Victor Laing and his staff at the Military Archives of Ireland and Airman Michael Whelan, Curator of the Air Corps Museum and Heritage Centre at Baldonnel.

For the chapter on the Fouga Magister in the Congo it was a rare privilege to meet the survivors of the Battle of Jadotville at the 50th anniversary commemoration in September 2011. We would like to thank John Gorman, Tony Roe, Bernard Sweeney, Martin Sweeney, Frank Donnelly, Danny Bradley, Professor Daniel Despas, Leif Hellstrom, Alf Blume, and Jean-Pierre Sonck.

The history of the Irish Air Corps Fougas that had previously been used by the Austrian Air Force was provided to us by Hubert Strimitzer and Josef Platzer and we would like to thank them both. Thanks also to Hans Ulrich Willbold of EADS and Patrick J. Cummins for sharing his extensive files and photos.

It was also a privilege to meet many current and former Air Corps personnel who provided us with a great deal of material on the flying aspects of the Fouga. We would like to thank Geoffrey O'Byrne-White, Myles Cassidy, John Flanagan, Kevin Barry, John Mulvanny, Paul Whelan, Graeme Martin, Chris Keegan, and Niall Connors.

For the engineering and maintenance aspects of the Fouga we would especially like to thank Paul Gibbons, Pat Cornally and John Hughes.

A special thanks to the Production Designer, Declan Maxwell who worked into the early hours to complete the layout and who learned a thing or two about the Fouga Magister along the way. Thanks also to Veronica Motherway for typing up the transcripts of the many interviews carried out for this book. Peter Hopkins deserves special mention for proof reading all of the chapters and suggesting useful changes that we have incorporated in the text. Thanks also to Barry Dalby of Eastwest Mapping for permission to use his map of Wicklow in Chapter 4.

Photographers and Photographic Collections

We would like to thank all those who generously provided us with photographs. Paul Fry, Kevin Byrne, Dave Corcoran, Paul Cunniffe, John Bigley, Fergal Goodman, Frank Grealish of IrishAirPics.com, Brian Pickering of Military Aviation Review, Peter Hopkins, Christopher Roche, Ricardo Hebmuller, Nico Braas, Magnum Photo Agency, Andrew Read, Robin A. Walker, Juha Ritaranta, Will Dempsey, Patrick J. Cummins, John Mulvanny, John McFarland, Peter Terlouw, R.A. Scholefield, Frank Donnelly, Hubert Strimitzer, Pat Cornally, Paul Gibbons and Graeme Martin. We would also like to thank Flight Sergeant Willy Barr and Sergeant Declan Parke of the Irish Air Corps Photographic Section for their assistance. Although not credited directly, we are sure that many of the Air Corps photos in this book were taken by these two photographers.

Finally we would like to thank our spouses, Margaret Farrell and Elaine O'Sullivan-Brinzan for their patience and understanding during the production of this book.

Authors' note

When we started this project over two years ago we had intended to produce a straightforward technical description of the Fouga Magister. However, as the research trail led us to unearth many almost forgotten facets of the Fouga in Ireland, the scope of the book became much broader. From the first major overseas missions by Irish troops on behalf of the UN to the Congo where the Fouga Magister was first encountered, to Ireland's fledgling attempts to start an aircraft manufacturing industry through foreign direct investment, the Irish Fouga story provides a thread linking seemingly disparate aspects of modern Irish history.

Almost forgotten too, is the incredible achievement by the Irish Air Corps Silvers Swallows Aerobatic display team in winning the prestigious Lockheed Martin Cannestra Trophy for the best flying display by an overseas participant at the Royal International Air Tattoo at Fairford in 1997. It was a phenomenal exercise in team work by a small cadre of dedicated staff and is an example of what can be achieved through hard work and good leadership.

Foreword
by
Brigadier General Paul Fry,
General Officer Commanding,
Irish Air Corps

Paul Fry
Brigadier General
GOC Air Corps

I first encountered the Fouga Magister type during the early stages of my cadet flying training course in 1975. My expectations had been to eventually fly the Vampire as an advanced trainer, but these hopes were suddenly derailed by a member of my senior Cadet class who informed me that the Air Corps had placed a contract for the purchase of six CM.170 Fouga Magisters to replace the old Vampire fleet.

A quick consultation of my Dumpy Book of Aeroplanes (1956 edition) produced an image of a small aircraft with a peculiar butterfly-tail, a twin-jet, with attractive sleek lines and tip-tanks. Apparently it lacked ejector seats and was armed with machine-guns rather than the bigger cannon of the Vampires. Anyway, they were new (to the Air Corps) and would probably be more serviceable than the older Vampires which were becoming a scarce sight in the air. We therefore could look forward to getting a lot more and better flying out of the Magisters on our Advanced Flying Training (AFT) course - if we ever got that far!

Delivery day came and the first two aircraft duly parked in front of Fighter Squadron's No. 3 Hangar, escorted in by two Vampires. The Magisters certainly delivered on being new and clean, but they were much smaller than the mighty Vampire where steps were needed to board the beast and yes, they didn't have ejector seats! But they brought with them better reliability and the bigger technical challenges of two engines, hydraulic systems, pressurisation, high speed and high altitude capability, that butterfly tail and its spinning characteristics and seemed set to deliver a real training challenge. Once we got into the air the challenge of all of these was indeed substantial, coming as my class did from the Chipmunk with no intermediate trainer to cushion the transition! In the air the difference was startling, the quiet and powerful response of the two engines and the overall smoothness of flight contrasting with the noise, clamour and smell of the Chipmunk. I suppose it was the final acclamation of the Chipmunk that it was a capable enough trainer to be able to produce jet-ready pilots!

Joe Maxwell and Radu Brînzan have crafted a readable and thoroughly researched book which I am sure will be enjoyed by all who flew the Magister, worked on it or even admired it from the ground. The history of the Fouga and the Defence Forces has dark origins in Central Africa where our first infantry battalions felt the lash of her tongue during their service in the Congo with the United Nations. Many UN Veterans are convinced that the Air Corps eventually operated one of the aircraft that attacked them and regularly examine Fouga 219 in the Air Corps Heritage Centre for battle damage repairs. The authors also cover in depth, the origins of the type, its name, other operators and include many first hand anecdotes relating to its handling and history in the Air Corps. Service in the Air Corps left very positive and indelible marks on the organisation starting, for example, with the high standard that it demanded from our Cadets and Officer trainees on the "Wings" Courses to those who gained experience forming, training and flying with the Silver Swallows. These skillsets were used during the set-up and development of the Beechcraft maritime patrolling operation of the 1970s as well as the new ministerial transport Service of the 1980s which evolved into the Air Corps deploying its aircraft with global reach. All pilots from 1976 - bar a very few - qualified on their AFT course through the Magister and, even when they graduated onto helicopter operations, the ingrained skills, work rate and airmanship demanded by this jet trainer enabled them to work to a standard which kept them ahead of the many complex systems fitted in these types. The type also kept our airspace very busy, advanced our maintenance skills and enabled the Air Corps' technical expertise to expand and embrace with confidence more complex types such as the Puma, Dauphin, Kingair 200, HS125 and Gulfstream models. The Magister has left a legacy which influences Air Corps' day to day operations ten years after it ceased training student pilots and technicians.

They say if it looks right, its flies right, and in the case of the Fouga Magister it delivered on both - very well indeed.

Paul Fry
Brigadier General
General Officer Commanding the Air Corps.

Chapter 1

What's in a Name?

The Fouga CM.170 Magister, known simply as the 'Fouga' by those who flew and maintained it, was an iconic jet trainer designed in the 1950s; the aircraft was operated by no less than 20 air arms, eight of which also used it as the mount for their aerobatic display teams. An explanation of the full designation of the Fouga CM.170 Magister gives some insight into the genesis of the aircraft, which was the first mass-produced, purpose-designed jet trainer to enter service anywhere in the world.

The Fouga company, which originally specialised in the repair of railway locomotives and the manufacture of railway carriages, was founded in 1920 in Beziers, in the south of France, by Gaston Fouga. The company flourished and within two years it was employing 2,000 people

at its workshops and saw mills. By 1936, Gaston Fouga was looking at new ways of utilising the woodworking skills of his labour force and with aviation in mind he turned to an engineer named Pierre Mauboussin.

Pierre Mauboussin had by that time already designed and built a successful range of light aircraft. As an initial foray into the aircraft industry, Gaston Fouga bought the design rights to Mauboussin's M120 two-seat trainer and touring aircraft. He also hired Pierre Mauboussin to work for his company, and together they developed the aircraft into the M.123 two-seat trainer for the Armée de l'Air; 65 were built prior to the Second World War and further examples were built after the war for private flying clubs.

The six Irish Air Corps Fouga Magisters on the flight line at Baldonnel. This photograph is undated but it is believed that it was taken in the summer of 1996 on the last occasion on which all 6 Fougas were fully serviceble and available for flight operations.
[Sgt. Pat Cornally Photo]

Prototype Fouga Magister. The production version differed by having a keel under the rear fuselage and constant taper wings.
[Joe Maxwell collection – Official French Air Force Photo]

Robert Castello was a talented engineer and draughtsman, who began his aviation career with Émile Dewoitine in 1922. He went on to work on many of that famous aircraft manufacturer's products, including the Dewoitine D.520, arguably the best French fighter at the start of the Second World War but built in too small a number to have any effect on the outcome of hostilities. Castello's own interests lay in gliders and he was to design a series of record breaking aircraft of this type throughout the 1940s and 1950s.

Fouga CM.8 R 13 Sylphe of 1950. Essentially a jet powered glider, this aircraft displays many of the key features of the subsequent Fouga Magister design including the 'V' tail and mid span airbrakes.
[MAR Photo]

Castello met with Pierre Mauboussin in 1939 to discuss the possibility that Fouga might manufacture his Castel 30S glider, which he had designed to be mass produced for use by gliding clubs. Castello had originally suggested the manufacture of his glider to Dewoitine, but that company's resources were directed towards the development of the D.520 fighter at that time. Mauboussin was open to the idea, but it was not until 1942 that the partnership with Castello was formalised when Fouga set up

an aviation subsidiary called Établissements Fouga et Cie. This led to the design of a series of powered aircraft and gliders all with the designation prefix 'CM', standing for Castello-Mauboussin. By 1944, the pair were senior figures within Établissements Fouga, with Pierre Mauboussin holding the post of Director of Aviation Services and Robert Castello acting as head of the design team.

Development of the Fouga CM.170 Magister

The late 1940s saw Établissements Fouga produce a number of innovative high performance gliders under the direction of Castello. New wing-mounted 'half moon' airbrakes were developed and these proved to be highly effective in allowing gliders so equipped to lose speed dramatically.

The Fouga company's glider designs came to the attention of Joseph Szydlowski, head of the engine manufacturer Turbomeca, who was looking for a flying test-bed for his brand new jet engines that were then under development. The new engines were low-powered and therefore a light airframe would be needed. The problem was discussed with Castello and Mauboussin at Fouga and they quickly came up with a variation on an existing glider design, the CM.8 15, which featured a 'V' (or 'butterfly') tail combining the control features of both rudder and elevators. Crucially, this design feature also placed the control surfaces away from the jet efflux of the engine, which was to be mounted above the fuselage in a similar manner to that of the Heinkel He 162.

The new engine test-bed was designated CM.8R 13 Sylphe and flew for the first time on Bastille Day, 14 July 1949, powered by a Turbomeca Pimene turbojet, which initially developed only a miniscule 0.83Kn (187lb) of thrust. The Sylphe allowed Turbomeca to test the engine under actual flight conditions and the company was able to quickly improve the design to provide an increased power output. Concurrently, the potential of mating an aerodynamically clean airframe with small jet engines to produce a jet trainer was duly noted by Fouga.

Based on their work with Turbomeca, Castello and Mauboussin proposed building a two-seat jet trainer for the Armée de l'Air designated CM.130R. The 130 part of the designation referred to the proposed wing area of approximately 13m² and the R stood for Reacteur (i.e. 'jet engine' in French). It was planned that this aircraft would

be powered by two Turbomeca Palas turbojets of 1.6Kn (353lb) thrust, but the overall design was deemed to be too small to fulfil the needs of the Armée De l'Air. Following further discussions with Szydlowski at Turbomeca, Castello and Mauboussin proposed an enlarged version of the CM.130R powered by two Turbomeca Maboré turbojets, each with an output of 3.9Kn ((882lb) of thrust. This aircraft was designated the CM.170R, with the 170 part of the designation referring to an increased wing area of approximately 17m². This proposal was accepted in late 1949 for funding by the Direction Technique et Industrielle (Technical and Industrial Directorate) and the design team at Fouga worked flat out to build the prototype. For its part Moraine Saulnier, who had a long history of supplying trainer aircraft to the Armée de l'Air, funded their own jet trainer design, the Morane Saulnier MS.755 Fleuret, to fulfil the Armée de l'Air requirement. Fouga was thus in competition with Morane Saulnier and in order to speed production of the prototypes, the construction of various components was subcontracted to other aviation companies including SNCASE (fuselage), Latecoere (wings) and Breguet (tail).

The rival Morane Saulnier MS.755 was also to be powered by two of the Turbomeca Marboré engines, which were still under development. To speed this process, Turbomeca once more turned to Fouga to provide flying test-beds for the new engines and this was accomplished through an innovative twin fuselage design using two glider fuselages joined by a common wing. The CM.88R Gemeaux (i.e. Gemini) was built in five variants to test various engines of differing power outputs, including the Marboré and Aspin, and proved to be essential to the early introduction of the production Marboré II into service.

The first flight of the Fouga CM.170R took place on 23 July 1952. The aircraft was highly distinctive in appearance, with its 'V' tail and high aspect ratio wings bearing witness to its glider ancestry. Flight testing went well until a fatal crash on 3

Left: A test bed for the Magister, The CM88 Gemeaux was an innovative way of testing two of the low power jet engines simultaeously by the simple expedient of joining two CM 8 fuselages on a common wing!
[Nico Braas Collection]

November 1952, caused by an attempted barrel roll at too low an altitude. There was some concern that the 'V' tail had somehow contributed to the accident and while it had always been planned that the second prototype would be equipped with a conventional tail for comparative purposes, it was somewhat timely when the second prototype (though actually the third CM.170R to fly) took to the air with a conventional 'T' tail on 6 July 1953. Comparison of the flight characteristics of both the 'V' and 'T' tailed versions indicated no appreciable differences in performance other than at high mach numbers, where the 'V' tail was more efficient aerodynamically.

The question of tandem versus side-by-side seating for military trainers has been settled in more recent times by the adoption of the tandem seating arrangement as standard. However, in the 1950s (and for some time thereafter) the debate would rage as to the merits of each type. In the case of the Armée de l'Air, the question was settled on 26 September 1953 when an order was placed for 95 production CM.170s, the side-by-seated Morane Saulnier MS.755 Fleuret having lost out, mainly due to the perceived disadvantages of this seating arrangement. By this time the Fouga aircraft had been named Magister, the full designation being Fouga CM.170 Magister. The production aircraft differed in many respects from the early

Left: The second prototype Fouga Magister fitted with a conventional 'T' tail for comparative purposes with the 'V' layout. There was no appreciable difference in performance so the design was standardised on the 'V' tail.
[Nico Braas Collection]

Fouga CM.175 Zephyr. This is the naval variant of the Fouga Magister equipped with strengthened undercarriage, an arrester hook and sliding canopies
[Joe Maxwell Photo]

Prototype CM.173/Potez 94 Super Magister. Designed as a follow-on to the standard Fouga CM.170 Magister with a completely new front end featuring ejection seats for the crew, a more tapered nose, wraparound windscreen and more powerful engines; the development of this variant was delayed by the diversion of resources towards the development of the civil Potez 840 turboprop executive transport. [MAR Photo]

prototypes. The most notable external differences included a wing of constant taper from fuselage to wingtip and a keel under the rear fuselage, which was designed to reduce the dihedral effect of the 'V' tail when rudder was applied. A small tail wheel was also placed in the keel to act in lieu of a tail bumper.

Production of the Magister was undertaken by Fouga along with Morane Saulnier, their unsuccessful rival for the Armée De l 'Air's jet trainer order, as prime sub-contractor; this was necessary because Fouga did not have the physical resources at their plant in Aire sur l'Adour to produce the aircraft in its entirety. In fact, Morane Saulnier constructed the majority of the airframe (including the wings) on the early production models, with Fouga producing just the front fuselage and cockpits at Aire sur L'Adour. Final

assembly was undertaken at a new facility at Toulouse-Blagnac. Training of Armée de l'Air pilots using the Fouga Magister began in June 1955; apart from a few teething troubles, including burst canopies at high altitude, the introduction into service went extremely well.

In 1956, Morane Saulnier wanted to free up some production capacity to allow them to develop their successor to the Flueret, the MS.760 Paris. To do so they reduced their participation in the Magister programme and the assembly of fuselages was contracted out to SNCASE, while Morane Saulnier continued to build the wings. The French Navy's air arm (i.e., Aéronavale) was also looking for a carrier capable jet trainer around this time, and to meet this requirement Fouga developed a suitably modified version of the CM.170 equipped with an arrester hook,

A four seat development of the basic Fouga design undertaken jointly by Potez and Heinkel, only two prototypes of the Potez-Heinkel CM-191 were built. [Robin Walker Photo]

Prototype of the much later Fouga 90 which failed to achieve any orders. This was the last development of the basic Fouga design. [John Read Photo via Andrew Read]

strengthened landing gear and sliding canopies. The prototypes of this variant were designated CM.170M (the M stood for 'Maritime'), while the production versions were re-designated CM.175 Zéphyr. With a growing order book, a naval version under development and studies for future specialised ground attack variants underway, the designers at Fouga were extremely busy, but cash flow became an issue for the company in 1956. The Fouga organisation based at Beziers had invested heavily in its aviation subsidiary at Aire sur l'Adour, but the financial effort involved in bringing the CM.170 into production threatened the existence of the entire company. With banks and other creditors demanding payment, an administrator was appointed and the decision was taken to re-structure the aviation subsidiary as a separate entity to be known as Air-Fouga, with a share capital of F.Fr75 million. Shareholders included Dassault, Breguet and Morane Saulnier and their involvement ensured that production of the Magister was able to continue uninterrupted.

The export potential for the Magister was given a major boost when the NATO Air Training Advisory Group recommended that the type be adopted as a standard trainer by all members of NATO. Although only France, Germany and Belgium complied with this recommendation, exports to non-NATO countries were highly successful and the order book grew rapidly with new orders from Finland and Austria as well as the aforementioned NATO members. The German company Flugzeug-Union–Sud built the Magister under licence, as did Valmet in Finland. Israel also ordered the Magister and obtained a manufacturing licence for the type. It is estimated that a combined total of 879 Magisters were built in France, Finland, Germany and Israel.

Variants and unbuilt studies

With the future of the company assured, Castello and his design team set about exploiting the full potential of the basic Magister design. This led to a series of proposed variants, some of which were actually built as prototypes, others remaining as paper studies. The initial production CM.170s had manual controls, but from airframe 168 onwards hydraulically boosted ailerons were introduced.

This modification did not result in a designation change. An improved version of the Magister designated the CM.170-2 Magister was produced

Potez 75 ground attack aircraft. The cancellation of an order for this aircraft by the Armée de l'Air was a bitter blow for Potez and led directly to the purchase of the Fouga company by Henri Potez. [R.A. Scholefield Photo]

Potez 840 civil executive transport. There were plans to build this aircraft in a factory at Rathcoole adjacent to Baldonnel. It was not a commercial success. None were built in Ireland and the failure of this project resulted in the demise of the Potez company, the assets being absorbed into Sud Aviation. [Juha Ritaranta Photo]

from 1960. It used a more powerful Turboméca Marboré VI engine. 137 of this version were built. Aircraft equipped with the original Marboré II engines were retrospectively referred to as CM.170-1 Magisters.

The CM.171 Makalu (named after a Himalayan peak) was a high altitude test-bed for Turboméca Gabizo engines, which provided four times the power of the Marboré II fitted to standard machines. This aircraft was fitted with metal canopies with side portholes to overcome the potential risk of bursting canopies at high altitude that had become apparent on some of the initial production CM.170s. The first flight of the CM.171 occurred on 5 November 1956, but the aircraft was destroyed in a fatal crash on 20 March 1957. The CM.172 was a proposed test-bed for Hispano Suiza R105 and R800 jet engines, but it was never built.

The CM.173, also known as the Potez 94 (more of which anon) was a 1962 design attempt to overcome some of the shortcomings of the basic CM.170 by providing uprated Turboméca Marboré VI engines of 5.2kN (1,168lb) thrust, pressurised cockpits and ejection seats. The aircraft featured a lengthened, more pointed nose cone and a frameless wraparound windscreen. Marketed as the Super Magister, the sole prototype flew for the first time on 9 June 1964 but no orders were forthcoming and the project was terminated in 1966.

The CM.174 was a 1957 design study based on the CM.170 but utilising a new swept wing combined with the principles of 'area rule' (a design technique used to reduce an aircraft's drag at transonic and supersonic speeds) developed in 1952 by NACA, the National Advisory Council on Aeronautics in the United States (the forerunner of today's National Aeronautics and Space Administration or

NASA). It was planned that the Marboré engines would be replaced by Turboméca Gourdon III engines providing 640kg of thrust. The aircraft was never built, but wind tunnel studies indicated that it would not have experienced the onset of compressibility before reaching a speed of mach 0.85, considerably better than the equivalent figure of mach 0.65 for the standard CM.170.

As already described, CM.175 was the designation used for the production navalised variant of the CM.170 built for the Aéronavale. However, to confuse matters, this designation was also used on a paper study for a single seat ground-attack variant of the CM.170 first proposed back in 1951.

The CM.178 was a 1958 study for a radically different-looking aircraft utilising most of the structural components of the CM.170 but powered by two turboprop engines mounted above the wings at mid-span. The spaces vacated by the Marboré jet engines would have been used to house two 30mm cannon in a proposed single-seat ground attack variant, but one again this project remained a paper study only, though the idea was resurrected briefly in 1960 as a proposed test-bed for the Turboméca Astazou turboprop engine.

The CM.191 was a 1962 joint venture between Potez (see below) and the German manufacturer Heinkel to develop a 4-seat version of the basic Magister airframe aimed at the military liaison and civil market. An aircraft of this type had actually first been proposed by Castello as early as 1949, but although two prototypes were built but no orders were received and the project was cancelled.

The Fouga 90 was a 1978 attempt to build on the success of the original Fouga Magister utilising the same basic layout but with a redesigned cockpit

featuring stepped seating to improve the view for the instructor, ejection seats and new avionics. The aircraft was powered by two Turbomeca Astafan engines of 7.6 kN thrust but failed to win any orders.

Fouga, Potez and the Irish connection.

Potez was a well-respected French aircraft manufacturing company first established in 1919. The company produced many successful civil and military aircraft up to 1940, though it was nationalised in 1936 and thus became part of the SNCASE (Société Nationale des Constructions Aéronautiques du Sud-Est) group.

Production of aircraft was halted during the war years, but the company was re-established as Société des Avions et Moteurs Henry Potez at Argenteuil in 1946 and went on to develop a successful range of industrial heating equipment. In 1952, the company started development at its own expense of an anti-tank aircraft armed with Nord AS-10 anti-tank missiles. This aircraft was designated the Potez 75 and although it was not successful in its intended role the prototype performed well during combat tests in Algeria as a counter-insurgency aircraft. An initial order for 15 of the type was placed by the Armée de l'Air in May 1956. This was later increased by 100 and Potez looked like it was about to re-enter the aircraft production business in a big way, but military budget cuts forced the cancellation of the order in May 1957.

Bitterly disappointed by this setback, Henri Potez nonetheless still harboured the desire to re-enter the aircraft manufacturing business, hoping to build a 4-engined executive transport to be known as the Potez 840 series. With this project in mind, Henri Potez purchased Air Fouga in May 1958 and renamed the company Potez-Air Fouga, later renamed simply as Potez. Following this acquisition, Potez had a ready-made design team that could be put to work on his planned civil executive transport. Existing Fouga design projects were renamed as Potez projects, the CM.173 for example becoming the Potez 94. Later some would argue that the CM.170 series suffered as a result of this re-orientation of the design team towards civil projects, as the Potez 94/CM.173 Super Magister did not reach the prototype stage until 1964. Had the Super Magister been available to replace the standard CM.170 on the production lines a few years earlier, it is entirely possible that some of the other projected designs such as the ground-attack derivatives may well have

come to fruition. Potez had already established a manufacturing plant in Galway on the west coast of Ireland to manufacture industrial heating products and was thus well known to the Irish authorities, who were keen to develop an industrial economy from one that in the early 1960s was still largely based on agriculture. With design work on the Potez 840 proceeding in France (the prototype had flown on 29 April 1961), Henri Potez approached the Irish government later that year with a proposal to build his new executive transport in Ireland. In February 1962, it was announced that an agreement had been reached with Henri Potez whereby two companies would be set up; Aviation Development Limited with a share capital of £3 million provided equally by Potez and the Irish Government and Potez Aerospace Limited, with a share capital of £500,000.

Aviation Development Limited was to be responsible for design and production of the prototypes of the Potez 840, the Irish government contributing the cost of the factory and the necessary tooling by way of its contribution to the company's share capital. Potez Aerospace Limited would appear to have been intended to take overall responsibility for the operation of the project. A site was chosen for a new factory at Rathcoole just outside the perimeter of Casement Aerodrome at Baldonnel, the main base of the Irish Air Corps on the outskirts of the Irish capital, Dublin. The plan was that the aircraft would be assembled in the new factory and test flown from Baldonnel, with a new taxiway linking the factory to the airfield. It was said at the time that the first production aircraft would be ready by 1964 and that eventually over 1,700 people would be employed at the site producing four aircraft per month.

The Potez 840 was planned as a 16-24 seat executive transport powered by four Turbomeca Astazou turboprop engines. The second prototype flew in France in June 1961 and this aircraft conducted an extensive 18-month sales tour in North America. Initially the outlook was positive and a production batch of 25 aircraft was planned, but firm orders were slow in coming and the company suffered a series of reversals when tentative orders were cancelled. While the Potez 840 was a fine aircraft, it was not what the market wanted in the mid-1960s, when jet-powered aircraft were in fashion. Companies that desired to have their own air transport at that time were much more likely to choose from the range of stylish executive jets being produced by Dassault in France, Lear in the United States or Hawker Siddeley in the UK than a more conventional-looking 4-engined turboprop aircraft. Attempts were then made to market the aircraft as a feeder liner for the bigger airlines, with advertisements taken out in aviation magazines proclaiming the Potez 840 to be the successor of the venerable Douglas DC-3. However, these marketing efforts were unsuccessful and only four production aircraft and two prototypes were completed, all in France.

Serious concerns were raised by the Irish government with Potez about their joint investment, when by 1964 the factory was completed but there were major delays in outfitting it with tooling and other equipment. During a visit to Dublin in 1964 Henri Potez alluded to the possibility of building jet aircraft, including the Magister and Morane Saulnier's Paris III, at the new factory at Rathcoole, but nothing came of these ideas. By 1966, public concerns were escalating into what was becoming a national scandal, with editorial comment in newspapers demanding an explanation as to where the Irish taxpayers' investment money had gone. Word was also filtering back from France that Potez appeared to be in financial trouble, with the announcement that no sales had materialised from the Armée De l 'Air for the Potez 94/CM.173 Super Magister. Potez were busy assembling the 6th and last batch of 140 fuselages for the standard CM.170, but there was no follow-on work in the pipeline. Some machinery was installed at the Baldonnel factory and aircraft components were made there but the workforce only ever reached a total of 113.

With the demise of the Potez 840 and no orders for the CM.173, it was inevitable that the parent company of Henri Potez would go into liquidation and by April 1967 its assets had been taken over by Sud Aviation in France. That year also marked the retirement of Robert Castello, the chief designer responsible for the development of the Fouga Magister. The name Potez passed into aviation history as far as full scale aircraft manufacture is concerned, though a subsidiary, Potez Engineering, remains active in aircraft sub-assembly design to this day. Interestingly, the name Fouga was resurrected

when Sud Aviation began a major marketing drive to sell refurbished second-hand Fouga Magisters during the 1970s. In June 1968, the Irish Minister for Industry and Commerce, George Colley made a full statement to the Dáil (i.e., the Irish parliament) about the Potez debacle. He explained that the Irish Government had contributed a total of £1,360,105 to the venture but that Potez had invested almost three times that amount (estimated at £3,640,000). The Minister went on to say that failure of the project was caused by rising development costs resulting in a substantial increase in the proposed sale price of the Potez 840, delays with the development of the aircraft's engine and crucially the emergence of other aircraft catering for the same market resulting in the loss of orders expected for the Potez 840. At the time that the Minister made his statement, the Irish subsidiary Potez Aerospace Limited was still in operation at the Rathcoole site undertaking sub-contract work, and the Irish Industrial Development Authority (IDA) had made extensive contacts with leading aircraft companies around the world with a view to enticing them to take over the operations at the factory, but to no avail. The factory closed its doors for the last time on 2 August 1968.

The facility was eventually acquired by Roadstone Limited, a cement products company, and in 1980 a new aeronautical venture was started on the site — the overhaul and maintenance of jet engines by Airmotive Ireland Limited, latterly called Lufthansa Technik Airmotive Ireland.

In 1970 Sud Aviation merged with Nord Aviation and Sereb to form the giant aviation conglomerate Société Nationale Industrielle Aérospatiale (SNIAS) with factories and maintenance facilities throughout France. When the Irish Air Corps was looking to replace their Vampire jet trainers in 1973 SNIAS was one of the companies that sought to fulfil the requirement, offering second hand Fouga Magisters. The company was renamed Aérospatiale in 1984 and was subsequently merged with DASA and CASA to form EADS in 2000.

Chapter 2

First Encounter

Airman James Galway (left) and Corporal Frank Donnelly (right) observe the arrival of Fouga Magister 92 of the Katangan Air Force at Kamina in 1961. Both were serving with the Air Corps Pipe Band (hence the kilts) as part of the 34th Infantry Battalion January-June 1961.
[Frank Donnelly Photo]

The first time a Fouga Magister was seen by Air Corps personnel was in February 1961, when Corporal Frank Donnelly and Airman James Galway were given the opportunity to examine the newly-acquired Katangan Air Force Fouga coded '92' at Elizabethville. Both men were members of the Air Corps Pipe Band and were serving with the 34th Infantry Battalion as part of the United Nations peacekeeping force in the Congo. Within a few short months, members of A Company, 35th Infantry Battalion would come under sustained attack by the sister ship (coded '93') to the aircraft sitting in the sunshine at Elizabethville.

In the 1960s there was a strong push for independence by many African nations from their colonial masters in Europe. Belgium had ruled a vast swathe of Central Africa known as the Belgian Congo since 1908. Prior to that, the region had been ruled exclusively by King Leopold II of Belgium as his personal fiefdom and was called the Congo Free State. The region was rich in rubber,

diamonds, copper, uranium and other minerals. The abuse of the indigenous population by the colonial power had been exposed by Roger Casement, the British consul at the time (and after whom the Irish Air Corps base at Baldonnel is named) and in 1908 the region was taken under the direct control of the Belgian government. By 1960, the clamour for independence by native Congolese had grown to such an extent that independence was granted quite suddenly in June of that year. However, the political and civil service infrastructure was run almost entirely by expatriate Belgians and when a rebellion by Congolese soldiers against their Belgian officers started within a few days of independence having been granted, many of the Belgian settlers were evacuated. This required the intervention of Belgian troops, who had only recently left the country. Amid this chaos, the mineral rich region of Katanga – led by Moise Tshombe and backed by the mining company Union Minière, with covert support from Belgium and other western governments – declared independence

Another view of the Katangan Fouga Magister 92. By September, the sister ship to this one (No. 93) would be engaged in attacks on Irish UN soldiers at Jadotville.
[Frank Donnelly Photo]

from the newly established Republic of Congo. The Congolese government called on the United Nations for support to help restore order, and the Irish government in turn responded to the UN's request for assistance in this regard from its member states. Ireland subsequently provided over 6,000 troops to the UN forces in the Congo from 1961 until 1964.

In January 1961, Lieutenant General Sean McKeown was appointed overall commander of the UN Forces in the Congo (ONUC), which included personnel from 24 countries. The original UN mandate was to oversee the withdrawal of Belgian forces from the Congo but this was later extended to include the expulsion of all foreign forces (predominantly Belgian and French mercenaries) from the country and to prevent the breakup of the state. The Secretary General of the UN, Dag Hammarskjold, appointed another well-known Irishman, Conor Cruise O'Brien, as his personal representative in the Congo.

Lieutenant General Sean McKeown (left), Commander of the United Nations Force in the Congo, and Dr. Connor Cruise-O'Brien, UN Representative at Elisabethville, photographed on the airstrip at Leopoldville's airport shortly before their flight to Katanga Province to confer with authorities there.
[UN Photo]

Since declaring independence, Katanga had been building up its armed forces with local troops known as Gendarmes, who were trained and led by Belgian and French mercenaries. A fledgling

air force was also established, utilising an eclectic mix of civilian aircraft. Katanga also ordered a total of nine brand-new Fouga Magisters from the manufacturer. The first three aircraft, originally destined for the Belgian Air Force, were taken directly from the production line, this short-cut in the procurement process being facilitated by Belgium's covert support for the breakaway Katanga. The three Magisters were partially disassembled and flown to Katanga in February 1961 on board a Boeing C-97 Stratocruiser aircraft operated by Seven Seas Airlines. The remaining six aircraft, which were still under construction at that stage, were eventually crated and put on board a freighter at Antwerp to make the long journey by sea to the port of Lobito in neighbouring Angola, from where it was planned to transport them by rail into Katanga.

In line with the UN mandate, Conor Cruise O'Brien instigated Operation Rumpunch on the night of 28 August 1961; this action sought to disarm Katangan troops, capture key Katangan military assets and arrest the foreign mercenaries forming the core of the Gendarmes. The operation was undertaken by Irish, Swedish and Indian forces in and around Elizabethville (later renamed Lumbumbashi), the capital of the Katangan province. The Gendarmes were taken completely by surprise on this occasion, and many of the mercenaries were arrested and subsequently deported. However, the operation was suspended prematurely by the intervention of the Belgian consul, who had undertaken to arrange the repatriation of the mercenaries, although in fact many of them were able to re-infiltrate the country within a matter of days.

Less than a week later, A Company of the 35th Irish Infantry Battalion was sent to the town of

Jadotville (later renamed Likasi), purportedly to protect the European citizens there against possible attacks by native Congolese. Jadotville was the headquarters of the Union Minière mining company, which was covertly backing the President of the breakaway province, Moise Tshombe. Nearby was the strategically important Shinkolobwe uranium mine, from which the ore used to construct the atomic bombs dropped on Japan had been extracted. When A Company arrived in Jadotville they found that the European population of predominately expatriate Belgians was openly hostile to the UN force, and that there was in fact no trouble between the Belgians and the local indigenous population.

Isolated by more than 120 km from the main UN forces at Elizabethville, the 156 men of A Company, under the command of Commandant Pat Quinlan, set to work building defensive positions around their headquarters at the Purfina garage in Jadotville. Commandant Quinlan sensed that trouble was brewing, given the large numbers of Gendarmes that were gathering in the area. He was not informed that back in Elizabethville, Conor Cruise O' Brien had decided to launch Operation Morthor on 13 September in another attempt to round up and expel all mercenary forces in Katanga. This time the Gendarmes were alert to the operation and fierce fighting erupted in and around Elizabethville between UN forces and the Gendarmes, led by their mercenary commanders.

A Company in Jadotville was attacked on the morning of 13 September by a force estimated at some 3000 Gendarmes. This battle, which has gone down in the annals of Irish military history, was to continue for five long days until 17 September, at which point A Company was forced to surrender due to lack of water, food and ammunition. They had inflicted hundreds of casualties on the Gendarmes with no loss to themselves. Most of the details about the Battle of Jadotville are outside the scope of this book. What is of interest, however, is that during the five days that A Company repelled daily attacks by the Gendarmes they were also subjected to repeated air attack by a lone Fouga Magister. This was one of the three aircraft that had been flown into the country back in February 1961.

A small team from Air Fouga had been sent to Katanga in February 1961 to train local pilots and technicians. Each of the three Magisters had by this time received Katangan Air Force markings (in the form of a roundel consisting of concentric rings of red, green and white, with three copper

crosses in the centre). They were also allocated the serials KAT-91, KAT-92 and KAT-93, though only the numerals were actually applied to the aircraft.

KAT-91 was destroyed in a fatal accident on 23 June 1961, when it collided with overhead power lines during a practice flight for Katangan Independence Day celebrations. By August 1961, most of the team from Fouga had returned home, leaving just one rated pilot in the country capable of flying the Magister. His name was José Magain and at the time he was a serving Belgian Air force officer acting as an 'advisor' to the Katangan air force. At this remove, very little is known about Magain – this, to say the least, is unfortunate, given that what is known would suggest that his story could easily provide the plot for a Frederick Forsyth novel. He was ordered home by his superiors as part of the agreement reached with the UN to end Operation Rumpunch, the rounding up of foreign mercenaries on 28h August 1961, but he refused to go. Instead, he set about arming one of the Magisters (KAT-93, based at Kolwezi) with machine guns and procuring locally produced bombs for use on the aircraft's underwing pylons. The other remaining Fouga (KAT-92) had by this time been captured by Indian troops at the airport at Elizabethville on 28 August and rendered inoperative.

Diplomats under attack. Conor Cruise-O'Brien dusts himself off minutes after the lone Fouga straffed a press conference in Elizabethville on 13th September in which Cruise-O'Brien somewhat prematurely announced the complete success of the UN operation to round up foreign mercenaries.
[Ian Berry - Magnum Photo]

The lone Fouga flown by Magain was to cause havoc among UN forces following the start of Operation Morthor on 13 September 1961, as no thought had been given by UN headquarters to any form of air defence for the troops operating in the Congo. Having destroyed several UN transport aircraft on the ground at Elizabethville airport during that morning, Magain went on to strafe the hotel at which Conor Cruise O'Brien was holding a press conference to somewhat prematurely announce the complete success of Operation Morthor! Contemporary press reports erroneously stated that the Fouga pilot was a Frenchman, Jacques Deulin, but in fact this was a ruse to hide the true identity of Magain. Deulin was actually the base commander at Kolwezi and had flown as a radio operator with Magain on some of the strikes against UN forces.

The Fouga that caused the havoc! Fouga 93 flown by José Magain that attacked UN forces in Katanga.
[Dave Becker Photo - Leif Hellstrom collection]

Locally produced bombs that were dropped by the lone Fouga on Irish positions at Jadotville and on the relief force at Lufira Bridge.
[Leif Hellstrom Collection - UN Photo]

On 14 September, Magain turned his attention to A Company, 35th Irish Infantry Battalion, who were surrounded at Jadotville. Following a high level reconnaissance flight over the area, he proceeded to bomb and strafe the Irish positions, this being the first time that Irish soldiers had ever come under air attack. They fired back with every weapon at their disposal, including FN rifles, Carl Gustav sub-machine guns, Bren guns and two water-cooled

Vickers machine guns mounted in Ford armoured cars that had been attached to the force. One round hit the Fouga near the nose wheel door but no significant damage was caused. Nevertheless, subsequent air attacks by Magain were flown at a higher altitude. Overnight on 14/15 September Commandant Quinlan made preparations to counter any further air attacks by having earth ramps built to enable the Vickers machine guns on the Ford armoured cars to have an increased elevation.

The author was privileged to meet with some of the veterans of A Company during the 50th Anniversary commemoration of the Battle of Jadotville held at Custume Barracks in Athlone in September 2011. Most of the members of A Company came from the area around that town, and it was not unusual for fathers, sons, brothers and uncles to simultaneously serve in the Defence Forces at that time. One of the veterans, Bernard Sweeney, recalled the air attacks by the Fouga.

"He kept missing us, which was the main thing, though every time he attacked we were rushed by the Gendarmes. I only had a Gustav, so I was kept busy firing at the Gends."

Bernard Sweeney was fighting alongside his two brothers-in-law, Private James (Jimmy) Redmond and Corporal Joseph Relihan in A Company, and there was much anguish at home caused by the propaganda emanating from the Katangans stating that the Irish troops had been overrun, with 50 dead and the remainder captured. Nothing could have been further from the truth – A Company was well dug in and had sustained a few wounded, but fortunately no fatalities. Sadly, this was not to be the case for the relief column under Commandant Johnny Kane, sent from Elizabethville on 16 September to attempt a breakthrough to the besieged A Company. The relief force – consisting of Irish, Swedish and Indian Gurkha troops – was held up at the Lufira Bridge on the road from Elizabethville and repeatedly attacked by the lone Fouga, resulting in the deaths of three Gurkha soldiers on 16 September 1961. Unable to cross the heavily defended bridge, the relief force had no option but to return to Elizabethville.

While the Fouga was attacking the relief column at Lufira Bridge, a UN Sikorsky H-19 helicopter flown by Norwegian Lieutenant Bihrne Hovden with Swedish co-pilot Warrant Officer Eric Thors made an extraordinarily brave but futile attempt to resupply A Company with water and ammunition. It was brave because they landed in the Irish position while under sustained fire from the Gendarmes, but ultimately futile because the helicopter had been

loaded with the wrong type of mortar rounds (81mm instead of 60mm) and the drinking water was contaminated, as it had been transported in Jerry cans that had previously contained fuel. The helicopter was unserviceable and could not take off again, and the two crew members would remain with A Company for the duration of their subsequent captivity.

In the firefight that erupted as the helicopter was landing, the Gendarmes exposed many of their previously concealed positions, resulting in their destruction by A Company. At this stage the Irish troops had fought the large force of Gendarmes to a standstill and it was the latter who requested a ceasefire on Saturday 16 September. With virtually no water, food or ammunition left, Commandant Quinlan requested orders from UN headquarters in Elizabethville while attempting to negotiate the terms of the ceasefire, but no clear orders were forthcoming. Commandant Quinlan was informed by headquarters that UN jets were on their way, but these never materialised. In fact, General McKeown had requested jet fighters as soon as the Fouga had started attacking UN positions in Katanga on 13 September, but the first of these (Ethiopian Air Force North American F-86 Sabres) did not arrive until 8 October, too late to influence the outcome for A Company. The ceasefire terms

that were agreed included the grounding of the Fouga, joint patrols with the Katangans in the vicinity of Jatotville and the restoration of the water supply to the Irish troops. However, by midday on Sunday 17 September the terms of the ceasefire had been violated by the Katangans with the Fouga flying overhead on several occasions and no water being provided to the Irish. It was under these circumstances and to avoid further loss of life that A Company formally surrendered. They were to remain in captivity until 25 October 1961, but were back in action again in December at the Battle of the Tunnel in Elizabethville.

A general ceasefire was arranged between the UN and the Katangans on 13 October 1961, but this was only to last until December 1961. The UN had been badly caught out with no offensive air support for their ground forces during Operation Morthor, and they remedied this problem with contingents of Iranian and Ethiopian F-86 Sabres, Swedish Saab J-29 Tunnans and Indian Air Force English Electric/British Aircraft Corporation Canberra B(I)8 strike aircraft. The lone Fouga was still at large, and it was rumoured – though never proven – that it may have been involved in the death of Dag Hammarskjold, the UN Secretary General, who had flown in a Douglas DC-6 to Ndola in Northern Rhodesia for peace talks with

A partial view of the Luluabourg airport, showing some of the Swedish Saab J-29 jet fighters that were placed at the disposition of the UN Force in the Congo (ONUC). Called "flying barrels", the jets were manned by members of the Swedish Air Force, numbering some 40 pilots and maintenance officers. [UN Photo]

Tshombe but was killed when his plane crashed there on 18 September. There was at this stage no sign of Magain, who had somehow managed to leave the country and return to Belgium. He flew for a commercial airline for a time and ran a successful business in Brussels. He never spoke publicly about his activities in the Congo before his death in 2003.

The Katangans built up their armed forces around Kolwezi and managed to procure additional aircraft in the form of T-6 Texans via South Africa (these aircraft were apparently ex-Belgian Air Force equipment).

When the ceasefire broke down in December 1961, the Indian Air Force Canberras flown by No. 5 Squadron were tasked with destroying Kolwezi airbase from which the Fouga had operated. They claimed to have destroyed the aircraft on the ground in their attack on the base, but it was more likely that they had only destroyed one of several well-made fabric and wood decoys that had been placed on the airfield. However, the Fouga was

Indian Air force Canberras deployed in support of UN forces attacked Kolwezi from where the lone Fouga was operating. Although claimed as destroyed, it was more likely that the Indian Air Force had destroyed some of the well made decoys that had been constructed around the airfield.
[Unknown Danish soldier - Alf Blume collection]

definitely damaged in the Indian attack and was subsequently trucked to Kisenge, near the border with Angola. After the end of the secession, it was evacuated to Angola and abandoned for years at Luanda airfield.

The secession of Katanga from Congo did not formally end until 1964 and during the period from December 1961 onwards there were many battles fought between the Katangan and UN forces in an escalating arms race that saw the introduction of air defence radars by the UN, following bombing raids on UN airfields by the T-6 Texans with which the Katangan Air Force had been re-equipped, and a foiled plan by Katanga to field over 40 North American P-51D Mustangs (sourced through an arms dealer in South Africa but assembled in Angola) against the UN.

As for the remaining six Fouga Magisters that had been transported to Africa by sea, the UN embargoed their delivery to Katanga and they were returned by ship to Antwerp where they remained crated on the dockside for some time. Over the years there were various rumours that they had been sold to Tunisia or Cameroon, but while four may have been, this was definitely not the case in respect of at least two of the aircraft. In a strange twist to this story, two of the aircraft once destined to be sister ships to the infamous KAT-93 that had played havoc with the UN forces in Katanga were subsequently purchased by the Irish Air Corps in 1974 and operated by them with serials 219 and 220.

In a final anecdote from A Company veteran Bernard Sweeney, he remembered that the Fouga gunfire seemed less accurate than its bombing runs; this recollection is actually supported by Professor Daniel Despas of the Africa Museum in Brussels, who after the end of hostilities was told by Jan van Rissegheim, commander of the Katangan Air Force that the guns in the lone Fouga had been placed 20mm too high in their mounts. This might explain the discrepancy between Magain's bombing and shooting accuracy, and may well have resulted in the saving of many lives in A Company at Jadotville.

TOP: Disabled Fouga at Kamina. This is most likely Fouga 92, which had been captured early in the fighting.
[Unknown Danish soldier – Alf Blume collection]

Above: Fouga Magister KAT 92 in dayglo and silver colour scheme. This is identical to the standard Fouga Magister colour scheme used by the Belgian Air Force at the time. This is not surprising as the Katangan aircraft were diverted from a batch produced for the Belgian Air Force.

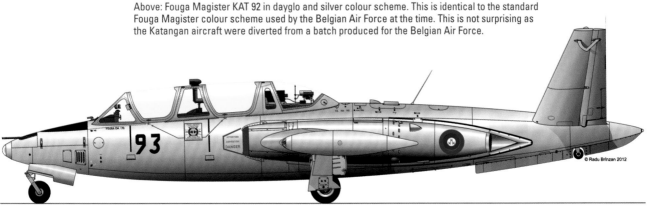

Above: Fouga Magister KAT 93 as used in the attacks on UN positions around Jadotville, Elizabethville and the Lufira Bridge in September 1961. It is believed that the aircraft which had the dayglo areas painted out.

Democratic Republic of Congo 1961

Chapter 3

Replacing the Vampire

The Air Corps had been operating the De Havilland Vampire T.55 two-seat trainer since 1956. This was a thoroughly modern machine when new. It was the tip of the spear as far as the Air Corps was concerned and it ushered in a new era of modern aircraft to replace obsolescent types that had been operated during the Second World War. The Vampires were operated by No.1 Fighter Squadron and the distinctive shape of the Vampire with its pod fuselage and twin-boom tail became a popular sight with the public due to their flypasts at annual Easter parades. From the mid 1950s, young cadets joining the Air Corps could expect to begin their basic training on a De Havilland Chipmunk followed by the Percival Provost, finally moving on to the jet-powered Vampire before receiving their wings. This training regime suited the needs of the Air Corps very well for many years, but by 1973 it was clear that the useful life of the Vampires was coming to an end. The

first generation jet engine had a low time between overhauls and there were difficulties in obtaining spare parts and repairing the combustion chambers, which were prone to popping rivets after only a few hours of operation.

In 1973, the Air Corps' Chief Technical Officer, Lieutenant-Colonel James "Jimmy" Teague, was tasked with finding a replacement for the ageing Vampires. Lieutenant-Colonel Teague is remembered by his colleague retired Commandant John Hughes as one of the best engineers he had ever met. Originally from Belfast, Lieutenant-Colonel Teague was working in Germany during the 1930s, but returned home at the outbreak of war and joined the Air Corps shortly thereafter. Conscious of the problems that the Air Corps was experiencing in maintaining the aged Vampires, and ever mindful of the stringent budget restrictions that were at the time a fact of life in

D.H. Vampire T.55 two seat jet trainer in service with the Irish Air Corps from 1956. The Fouga magister replaced the Vampires in service.
[Paul Cunniffe Photo]

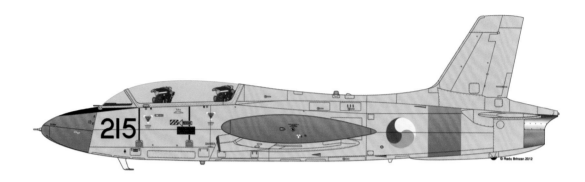

Aermacchi MB-326 in speculative colour scheme indicating how it might have looked had it been chosen to replace the Vampire instead of the Fouga. The type was evaluated in Italy in 1974.

Ireland, Lieutenant-Colonel Teague's priority was to find an aircraft that was both cost-effective and relatively easy to maintain. He drew up a shortlist of four types – the Fouga Magister, Cessna T-37C, Aermacchi MB-326 and BAC Jet Provost T.55. He compared the various characteristics of each type, including dimensions, engines, performance, armament and seating arrangements. However, of the four types, only two were subsequently fully evaluated, these being the Fouga and the MB-326.

By 1973, the Fouga Magister had been in service with the Armée de l'Air for over 15 years; as a consequence, most of the problems usually associated with the entry into service of a new aircraft had long since been resolved. Minor modifications had also been made to the aircraft and its systems as experience was gained on the type. Armée de l'Air personnel had expressed their immense satisfaction with the Fouga Magister to members of the Air Corps evaluation team that had travelled to France to conduct a thorough examination of the type. However, the negotiations with SNIAS were for the procurement of second-hand aircraft, and it became clear that not all of the machines on offer had received all of the modifications required by the Armée de l'Air and indeed some had not even come from the French production line.

An initial offer to supply six second-hand Fouga Magisters was received on 15 May 1973 from Henri Mollereau, the agent for SNIAS in Ireland (some references state 9 November 1973, but the author believes the earlier date to be the correct one). Four of the aircraft were of German manufacture, having 1200 hours on their airframes and 600 hours on their Marboré II engines; they were also described as being fitted with 'small ailerons'. These were offered at a price of F.Fr. 875,000 each (approximately €900,000 in 2012 prices). The remaining two aircraft were French-built and with only six hours flying time logged; they could therefore be considered brand new. They had a slightly different radio fit and were offered at F.Fr. 1,100,000 each. In addition, a spares package to the value of F.Fr.

1,000,000, including two spare engines, was also offered. Armament for each aircraft was to cost a further F.Fr. 250,000 per aircraft. This offer was rejected by the Air Corps when it became clear that the four German-built aircraft differed significantly in detail from their French-built counterparts. (The reference to small ailerons may have been a mistranslation as the author could find no evidence that German built Magisters were fitted with ailerons smaller than those on French built aircraft. It may have been a reference to aircraft which did not have hydraulically boosted ailerons.)

Although this initial offer was rejected, the Air Corps remained interested in procuring the Fouga and proceeded with the evaluation of this type, together with the Aermacchi MB-326, in early 1974. It is apparent from the relevant files in the Irish Military Archives that the BAC Jet Provost was also of interest to the Air Corps, but that company appears not to have responded positively to enquiries from the Irish authorities.

A team of Air Corps pilots and engineers was assembled to conduct the evaluation. Commandant Myles Cassidy (CO of No. 1 Fighter Squadron) went to the Aermacchi factory in Italy and on 10 January 1974 he had his first flight in an MB-326 (serial 54381) in the company of Colonel Bonazzi of the Italian Air Force. Commandant Cassidy recalled that the MB-326 was a lovely aircraft to fly:

"The MB326 was a single-engined aircraft powered by a Rolls Royce Viper turbojet. It was equipped with ejection seats and the particular one I flew was brand new off the production line. We put it through various manoeuvres demonstrating what it could do, flying in the general area of the Matterhorn on the Italian side of the Alps. I had a second flight in the aircraft later that day and we evaluated the general handling of the type and I found it to be a very pleasant aircraft to fly."

Five days later, on 15 January 1974, Commandant Cassidy flew an Armée de l'Air Fouga Magister (serial 473) in the company of Captain Lemarhollec

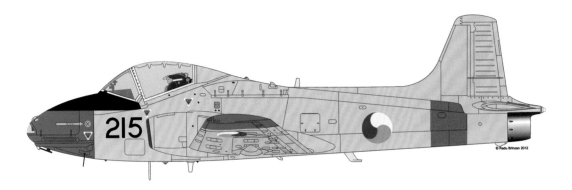

of the Armée de l'Air, followed by a second flight on the following day:

"It was our job to report on the two aircraft types as we found them, to describe their capabilities and to give the pros and cons of both. The final decision as to which aircraft would be purchased would be made by others. From a flying point of view, either aircraft would have been very suitable for the Air Corps."

Commandant John Hughes, who was part of the engineering team that evaluated the Fouga, recalls:

"There was a concern, given the difficulties we had been having in maintaining the Vampire, that whatever aircraft we chose had to be easy to maintain on a small budget. We were very concerned that we didn't want a 'hangar queen' on our hands, so we wanted to be assured that there would be plentiful stocks of spares available for the life of the aircraft, which we estimated would be at least ten years."

During the course of the evaluation, it became clear that if the Fouga Magister was chosen there would be considerable advantages in utilising the Turbomeca Marboré VI engine rather than the earlier Marboré II that was fitted to the particular aircraft on offer. Not only was there extra thrust available from the Marboré VI (an important consideration given that the Fouga Magister was considered by some to be underpowered), but the time between overhauls was doubled from 600 hours to 1200 hours.

On 22 January 1974, SNIAS provided a quotation to supply six Fouga Magisters to the Irish Air Corps for a total cost of £1,500,000. Some of the key terms of the proposed contract were:

- The six aircraft were to be refurbished to 'as new' and in accordance with the then current standard of the Armée de l'Air, including all modifications that had been introduced over the period of time that the aircraft had been in service.

- The aircraft were to be equipped with Turbomeca Marboré VI engines replacing the Marboré II's that were still fitted in the six aircraft on offer.

- SNIAS was to make full provision for the installation of armament, and this should be carried out without necessitating additional certification or modification of either the armament or the aircraft.

- The aircraft were to have an airframe service life of 2,400 flight hours (7 years) and 1,000 hours between overhauls on the engines.

- SNIAS was to certify that the work on the aircraft before delivery was free from defects and was carried out in accordance with all applicable industry standards then prevailing.

- SNIAS was to provide maintenance manuals and certification documentation in English.

- SNIAS also offered good financial terms, with payment being staged over a five-year period.

There is no record as to the exact offer price on the rival Aermacchi MB-326, but it was likely to have been well in excess of the £1,500,000 purchase price for the six Fouga Magisters since Aermacchi was offering brand-new aircraft rather than refurbished second-hand machines. On 21 March 1974 a deal was signed between the Irish Department of Defence and SNIAS head office in Paris for six Fouga CM 170-2 Super Magisters (the name Super Magister harking back to the advanced CM 173 of 1964, but in fact the aircraft purchased only used the engines proposed for that variant), with delivery of pairs of aircraft scheduled for November 1974, January 1975 and February 1975. On the day after the contract was signed, a French Air Force Fouga gave a spirited display to assembled guests at Baldonnel. A second display was flown over the Curragh Military Camp, Co. Kildare later that afternoon.

Previous Owners

The six aircraft offered to the Air Corps had interesting histories. Four of them had served with the Austrian Air Force (Österreichische Luftstreitkräfte). Purchased in 1959, the Fouga was operated by Austria until 1972, when it was

BAC Strikemaster in speculative Irish Air Corps colour scheme. Although of interest to the Irish authorities the company chose not to bid for the Vampire replacement contract.

Fouga Magister in service with the Austrian Air Force. Four ex-Austrian Air Force Fougas were purchased by the Air Corps after having been refurbished to as new standard by SNIAS. [Hubert Strimitzer Photo]

The Austrian Air Force used the Fouga as the mount for their Silver Birds Aerobatic display team in 1968. [Hubert Strimitzer Photo]

replaced by the multi-role Saab 105. The Magisters, having accumulated between 1,000 and 1,500 hours on each airframe while in Austrian air Force service, were sold back to SNIAS in part payment for Alouette III helicopters and were subsequently put up for sale by the French company. The first Austrian Air Force aerobatic team (known as the 'Silver Birds') was formed in 1966, flying four of the Magisters at air displays throughout Austria during 1967 and 1968, after which it was disbanded. Former Austrian Air force pilot Hubert Strimitzer was a member of the team and has fond memories of flying the Fouga:

"At that time, the training regime for pilots started with basic flying on piston-engined Piper Cubs followed by more advanced flying on the Zlin-126 or North American T-6 Texan. They then moved on to flying the jets. We used both the Fouga Magister and the De Havilland Vampire T.55. Our Fouga Magisters were never armed. Weapons training was conducted on the Vampires before selected pilots moved on to flying our first jet fighter, the Saab J-29 Tunnan. I flew in the number 2 position on the left wing of the Silver Birds and the Fouga was a beautiful aircraft to fly, though very underpowered compared to the Saab 105 that replaced it. There were no specific aircraft assigned to the Silver Birds, we just flew whichever jets happened to be available. In my log book I have records of having flown almost all of the Fougas at 25 different displays during that time.

After ten years or so it was decided that we should rationalise our fleet of aircraft, as we were flying a mixed bag of six different types. We chose the Saab Safir as a piston trainer and liaison aircraft and the Saab 105 jet as a multi-role aircraft, used as an advanced trainer, ground attack and reconnaissance aircraft all in one. We could even use it as a four-seat liaison aircraft by taking out the two ejector seats and replacing them with four ordinary seats. The Saab 105 was very powerful, but not as nice to fly in formation as the Fouga."

The Silver Birds were reformed in 1976 flying the Saab 105 and Hubert Strimitzer went on to fly with them, and with the later 'Karo As' display team before moving on to fly the Saab Draken interceptor, retiring from the Austrian Air Force with over 11,000 flight hours in his logbook.

The four former Austrian Air Force Fouga Magisters that were subsequently purchased by the Irish Air Corps originally wore the codes 4D-YJ, 4D-YK, 4D-YL and 4D-YU while in Austrian service, and from Hubert Strimitzer's records it is clear that all of these aircraft had been operated on occasion by the Silver Birds. As we shall see, they

would also become the mount for the Irish Air Corps' 'Silver Swallows' display team 20 years later; it is surely a rare occurrence that a single aircraft ends up being used by two different military display teams during its operational lifetime, let alone four aircraft.

The remaining two aircraft purchased from SNIAS had been part of a batch of six aircraft destined for Katanga in 1961, and in effect were sister ships to the aircraft that had been used on the attacks against Irish troops at Jadotville. However, they never made it into service with Katanga, as they had been the subject of a UN embargo. The aircraft had actually been transported by ship as far as Pointe Noire in Congo Brazzaville but were then returned to Antwerp. Eventually they came into the possession of SNIAS, who were busy selling refurbished Fouga Magisters throughout Africa, Asia and South America.

Châteauroux

The work to refurbish the six Fouga Magisters to 'as new standard' was planned to take place in the SNIAS facility at Châteauroux in central France. In 1935/36, Marcel Dassault built his first aircraft factory there, building Bloch bombers for the Armée de l'Air. After the fall of France, the factory was used by the Luftwaffe for the production of sub-assemblies for various German aircraft. The facility was bombed several times by the United States Army Air Force and the RAF during World War II. After the war ended, the factory attempted to re-start production for the Armée de l'Air, but by 1950 it was closed. In 1951, the facility was transferred to NATO for use as a depot and maintenance facility for joint use by the French and the Americans to support both civil and military aircraft; it subsequently became the largest depot in Europe supporting the United States Air Force and

other NATO air forces, with thousands of people working at the site. However, in 1966 French President Charles De Gaulle announced that France would withdraw from NATO's integrated military structure, and the United States was informed that it must remove its military forces from France. After the USAF's departure in 1967, Châteauroux was developed into a commercial airport, business jet centre and an aircraft overhaul facility.

It was to this facility that Commandant John Hughes and other Air Corps officers travelled to check on the work being carried out on the Fougas. As John recalls:

"There was an air of dilapidation about the place, you could still see the bullet holes and pock marks on the walls from the Second World War. It was clear that all was not well at the factory."

Less than three months after the signing of the contract to supply the six Fougas to the Air Corps, SNIAS headquarters in Paris had decided to close the facility at Châteauroux. This was to cause enormous difficulties for the Air Corps. The staff at Châteauroux were – quite naturally – not happy at the prospect of losing their jobs and a serious industrial dispute arose at the facility, resulting in extensive delays to the work being carried out on the Fougas. Commandant John Hughes remembers:

"Workers took it into their heads to occupy the management offices from time to time, literally sitting on the desks of their bosses in protest at the proposed closure".

With all of this disruption it was inevitable that the timetable for delivery of the aircraft would slip behind schedule, and as the planned delivery date of the first pair of aircraft came and went in November 1974 few could have predicted that it would be a further ten months before the first aircraft would arrive in Ireland.

Austrian Air Force Fouga Magister. 4D YL subsequently became 217 in Air Corps service.

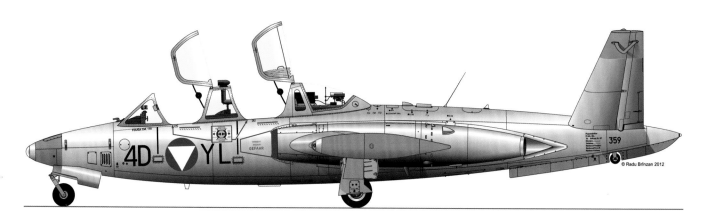

Delivery day. Irish Air Corps D.H. Vampires escort the Fouga Magisters into Baldonnel on 11 September 1975.
[Air Corps Photo Section]

Delays in Delivery

Patrick Donegan, the Minister for Defence at the time, was under pressure from the opposition parties in the Dáil to give an explanation for the delayed delivery of the Fougas and on 28 January 1975 he issued a statement confirming that the delay was due to production difficulties at the factory. It is interesting to note that in his statement the Minister also gave an account of order and delivery dates for two Alouette III helicopters ordered from another subsidiary of SNIAS during the same period that had been entirely satisfactory. One was ordered in March 1973 and delivered on 23 August 1973. The other was ordered on 3 January 1974 and delivered on 20 March 1974. Of the six Fouga Magisters ordered on 21 March 1974 there was as yet still no sign. The Minister made no secret of the fact that he was most irritated by the delays and difficulties being experienced in relation to the Fouga contract. The interminable delay dragged on throughout the spring and summer of 1975 and it finally became clear to the Air Corps that the Châteauroux facility was not properly equipped to carry out the refurbishment, lacking up-to-date manuals for the Fouga. Given the pressing need to get the aircraft into service before the remaining Vampires ran out of flight hours, it was reluctantly agreed to accept two of the Fougas without full certification. The armament of two

7.62mm machine guns had not yet been fitted to the aircraft and it was clear that there was no certification available at Châteauroux in relation to these weapons, or for the gun-sights, wing pylons and rocket pods. Finally, in August 1975 SNIAS wrote to the Air Corps informing them that two of the aircraft were ready for delivery. The acceptance party departed Baldonnel on 24 August 1975, but when they arrived at Châteauroux they found that the aircraft were not in fact ready to fly and further work needed to be carried out. Commandant Myles Cassidy and Captain Pat Cranfield (later to become the General Officer Commanding of the Air Corps) were the two pilots tasked with flying the two Fougas to their new home in Baldonnel. They were accompanied by Lieutenant Roger O'Shea and Lieutenant Kevin Humphreys. The pilots had completed a 7.5 hour conversion course on the Fouga nine months earlier at Clermont-Ferrand, but with an hour or two to re-familiarise themselves with the jet they were ready to undertake the flight home. (Note: While the pilots were being trained at Clermont-Ferrand, four Air Corps members undertook technical training on the Fougas. They were Captain John Nolan, Sergeant Joe Clavin, Sergeant Jim Fortune and Corporal Tom McHugh). The delivery flight was not without incident, as Commandant Cassidy recalls:

"We departed Châteauroux on 10 September with scheduled refuelling stops at Evreux in France and at RAF Lyneham in the UK. However, as we were taxiing in to the terminal in Chateauroux, one of the rudder pedals fell off the rudder bar onto the floor well of my aircraft and we had to wait for a technician, J. Blanchet, to come from the factory to carry out the repair.

Due to the delay caused by the rudder failure, we had to overnight at Evreux and the following morning

Fouga Magisters and D.H. Vampires overflown by Alouette 202 shortly after their arrival.
[Irish Independent Photo]

we continued the flight to Lyneham. After refuelling, we set course for Dublin and as we approached Baldonnel we were escorted by two Vampires of No. 1 Fighter Squadron, led by Colonel J.B. O'Connor."

There to greet them was the Minister for Defence, Patrick Donegan, and the Chief of Staff, Major General T. L. O'Carroll. Finally, after numerous delays and setbacks, the first of the six Fougas had arrived. Things were starting to look up for No. 1 Fighter Squadron.

Off to a Rocky Start

While the first two aircraft were in service by September 1975, further delays would hold up the delivery of the second pair until 16 February 1976. The technical staff at Baldonnel worked wonders to keep the two remaining Vampires serviceable so that students could get up to 10 hours each on them while other flight instructors were busy learning to operate the Fougas. It was a regular sight to see both Fougas and Vampires on

the Baldonnel ramp up to March 1976, at which time the Vampire was finally withdrawn from service. The fact that the Fougas could be operated at all was thanks to the assistance of the French military attaché, General Perrote, who – working out of the French embassy in London – provided translations of French flight and maintenance manuals into English. This should have been done by the company as per the contract signed back in March 1974, but despite assurances that they would do so they failed to ever deliver English translations of the manuals.

Within weeks of its arrival, the Fouga 216 was flying an operational role, helping to maintain an air cordon over the town of Monasterevin, Co. Kildare in conjunction with the remaining Vampires. The IRA had kidnapped a Dutch industrialist, Dr. Tiede Herrema, on 3 October 1975 and were demanding the release of three IRA prisoners as part of their ransom demands. The kidnappers and their victim were traced to a house in Monasterevin on 21 October and after a two week siege Dr. Herrema was released unharmed. During the protracted siege there was a very real threat that the IRA might try to infiltrate the area. Indeed, the IRA had in the recent past demonstrated a willingness to use hijacked helicopters for nefarious purposes, having attempted to bomb a police barracks in Northern Ireland from a helicopter hijacked in Co. Donegal. They had also hijacked a helicopter on 31 October 1973 and used it to stage a breakout of IRA prisoners from Mountjoy jail in Dublin by landing the helicopter in the exercise yard. With this threat in mind, No. 1 Fighter Squadron was tasked with maintaining an aerial cordon around Monasterevin until the siege was brought to an end. The Fouga Magisters that took part in this operation were unarmed. Retired Commandant

Cadets inspect the newly arrived Fouga Magister within days of its arrival. To the left of the picture visible between Cadet David Lannon and Cadet Kevin Byrne can be seen Monsieur Henri Mollereau, the agent for SNIAS. [Brig. Gen. Paul Fry Photo]

Fouga 216 on the ramp at Baldonnel on 6 November 1975. The VOR device had yet to be fitted as evidenced by the lack of nose antennae in this photo. [Paul Cunniffe Photo]

General Perrotte's personal aircraft at Baldonnel. It was thanks to General Perrotte, the French military attaché based in the French Embassy in London, that the Air Corps was able to obtain English translations of the flight manuals for the Fouga. [Brig. Gen. Paul Fry Photo]

Right: Collins VOR equipment installed in the aircraft by Aer Lingus engineers. This particular layout is unique to Irish Air Corps Fouga Magisters. [Joe Maxwell Photo]

Geoffrey O'Byrne-White was involved with this operation:

"What we were supposed to do in the event that a light aircraft or helicopter had tried to get near the siege house in Monasterevin I'm still not quite sure, but as is often the case our mere presence may have acted as a deterrent to anyone thinking of doing something like that."

The armament on the Fouga was to cause quite a few headaches for the Air Corps. Despite protestations from SNIAS to the contrary, it became apparent that the necessary certification for the 7.62mm machine guns to be used on the Fouga had not been carried out prior to the order being signed in March 1974 and there were difficulties in getting the guns to operate at all. Air firing tests as late as May and September 1977 showed that the guns were unreliable and prone to jamming, mainly due to the design of the ammunition feed mechanisms. Eventually this problem was resolved when a technician was sent from SNIAS to rectify the matter.

As the engineers and technical staff at Baldonnel delved into the inner workings of the new jets, it became apparent that not all of the work necessary to refurbish them to 'as new' standard prior to delivery had actually been carried out. Among the problems identified were worn flexible tubing connected to the pitot tubes and that agreed hardening of gears on the electrical generator linked to the port engine had not been carried out. Furthermore, it was clear that certification of the aircraft was an issue and – as already indicated – the Air Corps felt that the Châteauroux facility could not have had access to up-to-date maintenance manuals. These issues were raised with SNIAS by the Minister for Defence, Patrick Donegan and by Colonel J.B. O'Connor, and the company conceded that there were some problems at Châteauroux and that the remaining two aircraft would be overhauled by another subsidiary, SOGERMA, based in Bordeaux. SOGERMA was the main support organisation for all Fougas that were then operational with the Armée de l'Air and would therefore be entirely familiar with the aircraft. The final pair of Fouga Magisters was delivered from the SOGERMA plant on 13 November 1976.

Avionics Installation by Aer Lingus

It had been planned from the start that the Fouga would be fitted with modern navigation aids to Air Corps specifications. These included a 720-channel VHF radio and a VOR/ILS receiver with DME. The design and fitment of the avionics was overseen by Aer Lingus staff at Dublin Airport. Fouga 215 served as the pattern aircraft for the avionics installation and spent some months at the Aer Lingus maintenance facilities at Dublin Airport having arrived there on 22 September 1975. The avionics installation was completed six months later, the aircraft arriving back to Baldonnel on 22 March 1976. Thereafter the installation of the avionics took about six weeks per aircraft.

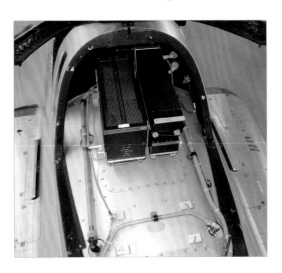

The Fouga is a relatively small machine and it took some ingenuity to get the electronics to fit inside the airframe. The bulk of the electronics were housed in the space behind the rear cockpit, aft of the pressure bulkhead and under the rearmost section of the clear canopy. The racks holding the electronic equipment are clearly visible through this section of the canopy and are of a unique design solely used on the Irish Fougas. Following this avionics upgrade, the aircraft carried a prominent semi-circular VOR antenna on either side of the nose.

Vampire and Fouga compared

Commandant Myles Cassidy had over 600 hours on the Vampire when he converted onto the Fouga Magister and was well placed to comment on the differences between the two aircraft:

"The Vampire was a first generation aircraft which had a long spool up time and was slow to respond to throttle movements. The Magister was slightly underpowered but it was a docile aircraft on which to carry out formation flying. The airbrakes were effective

and did not change the trim of the aircraft to any great extent when selected. The Vampire was more heavily armed, with two 20mm cannon compared to the two 7.62mm machine guns on the Fouga. The Vampire had side-by-side ejection seats, whereas the Fouga was not so equipped. In the event of an emergency in the Fouga you were supposed to jettison the canopies and bale out over the side with your parachute connected via a static line on your seat harness. Vampire or Fouga, neither escape system was very palatable. From an instructional point of view, we were used to sitting beside the student in the Vampire and being able to point out various features of the aircraft or aspects of the student's performance. The tandem seating arrangement in the Fouga took a little bit of getting used to and we

took some additional care over the pre-flight briefing as a result."

The issues around maintenance and after sales service came to a head in 1978, with a briefing note prepared for the Irish government describing a litany of defects (160 in all) that had been found on the six aircraft that had been delivered. The difficulties with the armament, provision of manuals and certification of the aircraft were described in detail. The issues were raised at inter-governmental level and the result was that all subsequent after-sales support would be conducted through the SOGERMA company. This was to prove a more satisfactory arrangement for all concerned.

Fouga Magisters and DH. Vampires operated concurrently until 1977. [John Bigley Photo]

Illustration of Fouga 218 as delivered, equipped with French radios.

The Irish Air Corps Fouga Magisters			
Manufacturer's Construction No.	Previous Operator ID	Irish Air Corps serial No.	Delivery Date
357	Austrian Air Force 4D-YK	215	11 Sep 1975
358	Austrian Air Force 4D-YJ	216	11 Sep 1975
359	Austrian Air Force 4D-YL (last flight by this aircraft in Austrian service was on 25 October 1971)	217	16 Feb 1976
390	Austrian Air Force 4D-YU	218	16 Feb 1976
298	Destined for Katanga but did not enter service	219	13 Nov 1976
299	Destined for Katanga but did not enter service	220	13 Nov 1976

Right: Route flown on the delivery flight of Fouga 215 and 216 on 10/11 September 1975. Two scheduled refueling stops took place at Evreux and RAF Lyneham.

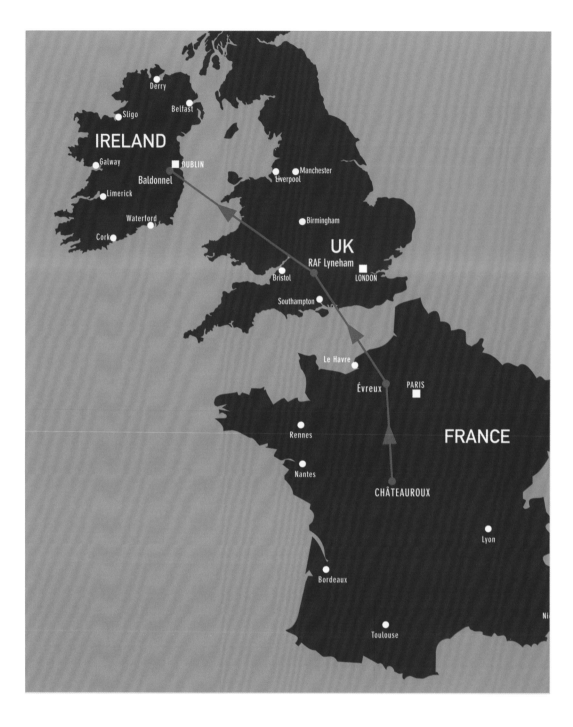

Chapter 4

Flying the Fouga

Fouga Magister high over Blessington Lakes in Co. Wicklow. During low-level navigation practice the Fougas could be seen skimming over the lake at extremely low altitudes trailing a wake on the surface!
[Air Corps Photo Section]

Despite the problems with initial service entry, the Fouga was a source of great pride for the personnel of No.1 Fighter Squadron. Retired Commandant Geoffrey O'Byrne-White recalls:

"I got my wings in 1975 and was immediately posted to No. 1 Fighter Squadron flying the old Vampires. There was a feeling amongst the Air Corps that helicopters were the big thing. The Alouettes, which had been in service since 1963, were very successful and had a high profile with the public and we had technical staff transferring out of No. 1 Fighter squadron to go and work on the helicopters. With the arrival of the Fougas in 1975 all that changed. We had dedicated and committed staff putting a lot of work into the new jets. The Fougas were a source of great pride to those who flew and maintained them, particularly so a few years later when the Silver Swallows aerobatic display team got going".

Although the Fougas was operated by No. 1 Fighter Squadron, they were shared on an 'as needed' basis with the Advanced Flying Training School when 'Wings' courses were being held. As experience in operating the Fouga grew, each class flew more hours on the type. The five cadets of the 9th Regular Air Corps Cadet Class graduated in September 1976 and they had flown 40 hours each on the Fouga. The following class did nearly 100 hours each as there were only three students for six aircraft. The 11th Regular Cadet Class of 1977 went back a step and only logged ten hours each on the Fouga as there were 14 students that year. The Fouga had replaced the Vampire in the advanced training role and the Air Corps similarly replaced the Chipmunk/Provost combination in the basic flying training role with the SIAI Marchetti SF260WE Warrior, the first of these arriving in 1977. The combination of Marchetti/Fouga for the flying training syllabus was to last for more than 20 years until the withdrawal of the Fouga in 1999. The Marchetti was operated by the Basic Flying Training Squadron (BFTS) and students were expected to complete 150 hours on this type before moving on to the Fouga for a further 50 hours in order to complete the 'Wings' course.

Interesting picture showing two future General officers Commanding the Air Corps. From left to right, Cadet Nick McHugh, Commandant Myles Cassidy, Commandant Pat Cranfield and Cadet Paul Fry. Cadet McHugh became the first cadet to go solo on the Fouga by virtue of the fact that he got to the runway threshold slightly ahead of Cadet Fry! [Air Corps Photo Section]

The Fouga Magisters participated in their first major public display on 26 August 1979 when 216, 218, 219 and 220 flew a formation flypast at the 'Air Spectacular' event held at Fairyhouse Race Course. Although no aerobatics were flown at this stage, this was to be the first of many appearances by the Fougas at air displays at home and abroad.

In September 1979 the Air Corps was heavily involved in the preparations for the visit of Pope John Paul II to Ireland and the Fougas were seen by the largest crowd ever assembled in one location in Ireland. Over one million people had gathered in the Phoenix Park in Dublin for a mass to be celebrated by the Pope on the first day of his three day visit. The Aer Lingus Boeing 747 carrying the Pope

overflew the Phoenix Park in the company of an escort consisting of four Fouga Magisters flown by Commandant Paddy Curley, Officer Commanding No.1 Fighter Squadron, Captain Barry Murphy, Lieutenant Nick McHugh and 2nd Lieutenant Tony Regan. Commandant Paddy McNally was acting as observer in the rear seat of the lead Fouga and after the 747 had landed at Dublin airport the four escorting Fougas were joined by a fifth flown by 2nd Lieutenant Dermot McCarthy. The five aircraft flew a cross formation over the crowd at the Phoenix Park before heading back to Baldonnel.

Tactical flying

In 1980, following a re-organisation of the Air Corps, No. 1 Fighter Squadron became Light Strike Squadron, a name more reflective of its actual role. Captain John Flanagan became Acting Officer Commanding Light Strike Squadron in 1981 (John later became Officer Commanding Light Strike Squadron on his promotion to Commandant in 1983) and started to devise the tactics that would be required to utilise the Fouga in an operational ground attack role should the need arise. The Israelis had used the nimble Fouga in the ground attack role during the 1967 and 1973 conflicts with Egypt and Syria; the Katangan use of the Fouga in a similar role against Irish troops back in 1961 was described in Chapter 2. John describes the operation of Light Strike Squadron at that time:

"I had spent two very enjoyable years at Gormanston as an instructor with Army Co-Operation squadron before returning to Baldonnel as an instructor with BFTS. At that time it was only the instructors who flew the Fougas on a regular basis, and then only when there was a Wings course running. The Fouga rated instructors were often working back in BFTS as and when needed, so it was a very flexible use of available manpower. When I was designated as Acting Officer Commanding of Light Strike Squadron I was the only pilot permanently assigned to the squadron. That situation continued for a few years with my staff of instructors moving back and forth between BTFS and Light Strike Squadron. I felt very strongly that there needed to be new pilots assigned to Light Strike Squadron on a full-time basis. I asked for, and was assigned, two very capable men straight from their 'Wings' course in 1984, Lieutenant John Kelly and Lieutenant John Mulvanny and I couldn't have asked for two brighter or more talented people. I had my own ideas about tactical flying and I told the two lads to come up with ideas of their own and we would put it all in the mix. I wanted to design a proper operational conversion course for the Fouga that would include low-level navigation, night flying, formation flying, air firing and generally getting involved with supporting the Army.

One of the first things we needed was a designated area for low flying relatively close to Baldonnel. The old route was fine for slower aircraft. I experimented with a route through the Dublin and Wicklow Mountains. We needed an area free of power lines and other obstacles and not too close to hospitals or other sensitive areas".

This low-level training route through Wicklow was subsequently used for many years until the advent of the longer-ranged Pilatus PC-9 made possible the use of low level flying areas in the West of Ireland away from populated areas:

"We also did a lot of air firing at targets using the 7.62mm machine guns and the SNEB 68mm rockets. The range was on the beach at Gormanston and the targets in my time consisted of old wooden cable drums procured from the ESB or Telecom Eireann [respectively the Irish electricity supply and telecommunications companies at the time], filled with foam and painted dayglo orange. We wanted to develop tactical flying to support army operations and while our accuracy was very good at Gormanston, unfortunately we were never able to get permission to do live firing at the Army's main shooting range in the Glen of Imaal in County Wicklow".

Retired Commandant John Mulvanny was the young Lieutenant referred to in John Flanagan's account of Light Strike Squadron and tactical flying. John Mulvanny subsequently went on to be a flying instructor in 1987 and leader of the Silver Swallows aerobatic team in 1990. John has his own perspective on that particular time:

"The route we flew for low-level navigation practice took us out of Baldonnel, down across the Blessington Lakes before turning left and running through the Wicklow Gap and down the valley to Laragh. We took a hard right turn at Laragh, down past Rathdrum and out to the coast at Arklow, where we headed south towards Wexford. We would then do a U-turn and come back as far as Laragh, avoiding the noise sensitive Glendalough Valley. Instead of turning left and going back up the Wicklow Gap, we would fly straight ahead and keeping low, follow the valley up to the Glenmacnas Waterfall, pulling up at the last minute, half rolling inverted to avoid going too high at the top of the waterfall, then rolling back right way up, before trying to follow all the

With such a small fleet it would be normal to have one or two aircraft unavailable due to servicing requirements as the various hourly checks came due but on one occasion on 14th April 1981 all six Fouga Magisters flew together. The pilots who flew the aircraft on this occasion were Lieutenant Andy O'Shea, Lieutenant Dermot McCarthy, Lieutenant Tony Regan, Captain Con Murphy, Captain Geoffrey O'Byrne White and Commandant Paddy Curley.
[Air Corps Photo Section]

Another rare photo, this time showing Fouga 216 adorned with the Light Strike Squadron badge on 20 May 1983.
[Fergal Goodman Photo]

The original No.1 Fighter Squadron badge dating from the early 1940s on which the Light Strike Squadron badge was based. The key difference was the lack of text on the scrolls in the 1983 version. Beag ach fiachmar translates as Small but Fierce.

twists and turns of the Military Road as far as the Sally Gap. You couldn't really manage to follow each and every twist of the road as we were doing about 300 knots. Then we would make a hard left turn at Sally Gap and follow the valley back down to Blessington lake, before turning for Brittas Gap and back to Baldonnel. I remember on one occasion surprising a motorist who had stopped his car at the Sally Gap. It's fairly flat up there and he hadn't seen me coming. You didn't tend to hear the Fouga until the last second when it' was doing 320 knots and I remember the startled look on his face as I passed him barely sixty yards away".

This was not the only occasion on which the Fouga was to fly extremely low. As John Flanagan recalls:

"I have fond memories of flying low over the Curragh where the Army had set up their then new Giraffe mobile radar and Bofors RBS 70 surface-to-air-missiles. The Curragh is a vast plain with only a few low hills. They had placed the radar on a hill and they asked us to act as targets so that they could track us. Well, they could neither track us on radar nor see us visually on our first run. Captain Tony Regan was my wing man and we had flown up the hill! We then did a few circuits to give the operators some chance of tracking us before heading back to Baldonnel. I heard afterwards that a few senior officers had lost their berets when they dived for cover during our first run".

Commandant John Flanagan together with Lieutenant John Kelly and Lieutenant John Mulvanny developed the operational conversion course for the Fouga and naturally enough this included a substantial amount of air firing.

As John Mulvanny recalls:

"I've been very lucky, along with John Kelly, I've have probably done more air firing in Fougas than anyone else. We managed to fire an awful lot of 68mm rockets as they were coming close to being time-expired and would have to have been disposed of anyway. We were trying to develop into what ultimately Light Strike Squadron should have meant, in that if the Army requested air support for an operation we could provide it. We developed the Operational Conversion Course to cover these tactics, practicing low-level loose formation navex's, [navigational exercises] leading into the IP (initial point) where we'd pull up, acquire the target, fire and get out again, basically using the aircraft in much the same way as the Israelis had done in 1967. We did carry out many exercises with the Army and Navy but it was more for their benefit in learning how to deal with an air attack rather than combined operations we had trained for, where they would call for air support from a tactical formation of Fougas".

Although the Fouga Magister was relatively low-powered, that didn't hinder the tactical use of the aircraft too much. As John Mulvanny explains:

"The relative low power available on the Fouga was a limitation in formation aerobatics but anything you wished to do in tactical flying you could perform at the maximum capability of the aircraft. For example, we were always trading off speed versus endurance. We flew Dublin to Cork airport in 17 minutes on one occasion at full power but we probably only had an endurance of 25 minutes at that power setting. The normal endurance of the Fouga was somewhere between an hour and an hour and a half depending on what power setting you were using. A normal navex would be carried out with the engines running at 18,500 rpm out of a maximum of 21,500 rpm available.

Formation aerobatics were carried out at 19,500 rpm. If you are operating the aircraft as a singleton you can only do what the aircraft is capable of. Comparisons with other aircraft don't come into it. Of course, had we operated in conjunction with other types of aircraft then you can make comparisons and wish you had more power or a higher roll rate, etc. From a tactical survival point of view you should operate the aircraft to the very edge of what it's capable of doing. We were very fortunate in having John Flanagan as OC. He was all on for us to operate the Fouga to the maximum of its capability and as a twenty-year-old flying a nice twin engine jet it was absolutely brilliant!"

Military Exercises

As the years progressed, the training value of having jet aircraft available for exercise scenarios came to be appreciated by the Army, which had a long-standing commitment to UN peacekeeping operations in Lebanon. Irish troops were part of the UNIFIL force based in south Lebanon close to the border with Israel and when trouble flared between warring factions in the region it was not uncommon for bomb strikes to be carried out by Israeli aircraft in the Irishbatt area of operations. The Army realised that it would be useful if troops working up for their overseas deployment could be exposed to simulated air attack as part of their training. As Commandant Paul Whelan explains:

"To provide training for troops going overseas on UN missions we flew simulated air attacks over the Glen of Imaal army range, usually upon 'dug-in' troops on exercise. These were usually planned in advance with the Corps of Engineers. As live firing from aircraft was not permitted over the Glen at that time, the Engineers used a series of HE (High Explosive) charges. These charges were buried at safe distances from the trenches, yet close

Commandant John Flanagan rolls away from the camera ship to provide an excellent view of the two Matra rocket pods mounted under the wings. [Air Corps Photo Section]

The Siai Marchetti SF 260W Warrior was the basic trainer used operated by Basic flying Training School. Students would progress from the Marchetti onto the Fouga. It was a versatile aircraft, seen here armed with Matra Rocket pods at Waterford Airport.
[Patrick J. Cummins Photo]

enough to simulate a 'strafing run' by an attacking aircraft. We would meet with the exercise co-ordinators and the engineers to plan the entry and exit points for the simulated attack. The 'runs' between these points would coincide with the orientation of the laid HE charges. As we passed over the dug in positions, the engineers would flick a series of toggle switches on a control board which realistically simulated a strafing run".

Indeed, it was not just the Army that benefitted from the participation of the Fougas on military exercises. The Fougas participated in a number of notable naval exercises down through the years including Exercise 'Dan Buoy IV' in September 1981 in which a pair of Fougas staged mock attacks on Irish naval vessels operating in the Irish Sea. A similar exercise was carried out in September 1992 code-named 'Red Tide' during which two Fougas flying from Cork Airport staged mock attacks on naval vessels operating off the Old Head of Kinsale on the south coast of Ireland. The current General Officer Commanding the Air Corps, Brigadier General Paul Fry, was the Forward Air Controller on that exercise.

"We spent a week enduring Force 8 gales doing 8 knots with six other naval ships for company. On the day of the air attack there were warm sector conditions (low cloud, slight rain or drizzle) and the Light Strike crews did really well to surprise the flotilla, flying a low altitude approach and using the backdrop of the coast to mask them from the ships radars".

Learning and Instructing on the Fouga

Having completed 150 hours of flying on the Marchetti, students would move on to the Fouga to complete their training. John Mulvanny explains the philosophy behind the training on the Fouga.

"The Marchetti was a fantastic training aircraft and far more difficult and exacting an aircraft to fly well when compared with the Fouga. If you were a good pilot it [the Marchetti] allowed you to shine but if you weren't so good it would bite you back. By the time a student had 150 hours on the Marchetti, the Fouga didn't offer any real new difficulty in terms of handling. But it was a faster aircraft and it was twin-engined, so we used those characteristics to put the students under a different form of pressure by operating at a relatively high speed. So for example, standard re-entry to the circuit would be over the initial point, but always at 300 knots, then break, and position downwind to land. Things happen fast at 300 knots so the student always had to be thinking ahead. The Fouga provided us with that capability to get the guys to think ahead and it was a great way to finish off a 'Wings' course. We could also practice single engine approaches and dealing with unexpected power loss due to simulated engine failure in the Fouga. The engines were mounted so close to the centreline that there wasn't any appreciable asymmetric movement when you throttled back one engine but it was still a valuable training experience to deal with the loss of an engine".

Commandant Paul Whelan is also a former instructor on the Fouga and member of the 1997 Silver Swallows team, and currently flies the Gulfstream GIV. A sport parachutist as a teenager until an in-flight technical failure of an old parachute design caused him to consider other less hazardous ways to enjoy flying, Paul joined the Defence Forces in November 1989 and graduated from the Cadet School eighteen months later with the rank of 2nd Lieutenant. Paul commenced the 'Wings' Course in 1991 and graduated from that course in 1992. As mentioned above the 'Wings' syllabus consisted of 150 hours on the Siai Marchetti SF260WE Warrior and 50 hours on the Fouga. But as Paul explains the course was modified somewhat during his training.

"We were the first class to fly the SF260D model of the Marchetti, the so called 'white Marchettis' leased in from the USA to cover a temporary shortage of training aircraft. The SF260D was used as a flight screener at Gormanston Air Station, Co. Meath where we flew 10 hours on the type. Of the 15 Young Officers on the course, six were removed after the initial 10 hours and nine continued training on the Marchetti SF260WE model with one more YO (Young Officer) leaving us a bit later. At the 100 hour stage the class was split in two, four of us going onto the Fouga and the other four continuing with the SF260. After a further 50 hours we swapped so that by the time the course was completed each of us had 150 hours on the Marchetti and 50 hours on the Fouga. The reason for the split at the 100 hour stage was due to instructor and aircraft availability. It was easier to concentrate on four students at a time on each type but both groups trained simultaneously."

The 50 hours on the Fouga consisted of a series of lessons on basic handling, circuits and emergencies, rate 1 turns (360 degrees in 2 minutes), climbing and descending, climbing and descending turns, stalls and spin recoveries, aerobatics, navigation exercises, high-altitude flight and instrument flying. Once a discipline was mastered with the instructor, it was carried out solo (with the notable exception of spinning, an exercise considered too hazardous for solo students in the Fouga. Solo spinning, was however, performed in the Marchetti).

The key difference between the Marchetti and the Fouga from an instructional point of view (apart from the obvious single piston versus twin jet) was the side-by-side seating in the Marchetti giving way to the tandem arrangement in the Fouga. As Paul explains:

"Coming from the Marchetti you could get a good vibe from the mannerisms and the body language of the instructor sitting beside you as to how well or not you were doing. The Marchetti was an easier aircraft to fly from an ergonomic point of view. That said, when you

walked out to a Fouga for the first time with your seat parachute awkwardly banging off the backs of your knees, everything felt really cumbersome and uncomfortable. But as soon as you slotted your parachute into the bucket seat, secured your notes and charts, and fastened your five-point harness, you immediately felt as if you became part of the machinery. Because of the confines of the Fouga, the cockpit is small, almost claustrophobic; everything is very close to your fingertips. It had to be, as you didn't have much elbow-room either. In fact the Fouga was one of the reasons we had height restrictions on pilots joining the Air Corps for a long time. It really is quite small. It is also close to the ground and you felt very close to the front of the aircraft with the wings behind you but mainly you felt as if you were part of the aircraft.

In the Fouga we didn't have the luxury of side-by-side seating, all you had was the instructor's voice in your ear. There were stories from the old days of some instructors using golf clubs to reach forward and tap the student on the shoulder but thankfully that didn't occur during my time. In fact the only body language you could sense from the instructor was their follow-through on the controls, you could sense their feet on the rudder pedals or their hands moving on the controls. Often it was more than you might like. Sometimes I would land the aircraft and wonder did I actually land that? You would imagine that if I took my hands away at the last second the instructor would land it perfectly well and still say that I had made a great landing! Coming from the Marchetti, which was notoriously difficult to land because the nose wheel landing gear hung lower than the main gear when straight and level (so if you didn't have a definitive roundout and a flare on landing the nose wheel would touch down first and you would bounce back up) the Fouga landing routine was relatively uncomplicated, very little if any flare or round-out required. It was more of a 'check' back pressure on the control column and you had done enough to secure a reasonable landing".

As training progressed and solo flights were undertaken, one of the flights was called the compressibility run. As Paul recalls:

"One of the things that told you were really alone in this jet was the high altitude compressibility run where we would take the aircraft up to 25 to 30,000 feet and spend all day getting there. You would get to 16,000 feet no problem but above that altitude the performance was quite low and you might only manage a rate of climb of between 300 to 400 feet per minute, sometimes less. But once you got to that altitude in that whistling jet, the whistling became very quiet and you really felt quite isolated. You became very conscious that there was only a thin canopy between you and no oxygen should a problem arise. Once you reached 30,000 feet you literally rolled over, pushed the nose down until you reached a speed of 300 knots and then you popped out

The elegant lines of the Fouga Magister are clearly shown in this plan view.
[Air Corps Photo Section]

the airbrakes and maintained that speed all the way down to 10,000 feet in what was in effect an emergency descent. The maximum speed of the Fouga was Mach 0.82 but we generally never went above Mach 0.8.

One of the key milestones for any student pilot flying the Fouga was gaining their instrument rating on the type. It was not a standard 'T' style instrument layout in the Fouga cockpit and the instruments were old (some notated in French, adding to the uniqueness of the aircraft). "You sat in the rear cockpit with the fabric instrument flying canopy pulled forward so you couldn't see out and you really had to hone your skills to keep your scan going as it wasn't easy to move from VSI to altimeter to airspeed to turn and slip to heading. To achieve your instrument rating you really had to nail this, probably in a more difficult way than you would have had to do in say, the Marchetti. There was no ground simulator for the Fouga on which to practice on, so apart from studying the manuals and course notes all of this was done in the air.

A low-flying Fouga buzzes the Control Tower at Baldonnel. Note the WWI vintage hangars in the background.
[Lt. Col. Kevin Byrne Photo]

Fouga 216 gets the wheels up smartly during a formation takeoff.
[Air Corps Photo Section]

We practiced emergency drills in the circuit including hydraulic failure by switching off the hydraulic system. You would then attempt to put down the landing gear but nothing would happen. Standing out on the ramp watching emergency circuits you could always tell who was putting the landing gear down using the emergency hydraulic system. There was a big lever on the right hand side of the cockpit for this and you had to swap hands – putting your left hand on the control column to maintain straight and level while pumping the gear down with your right. You could see the aircraft oscillating up and down slightly as the pumping action of the right hand was transmitted across to the left hand which wasn't used to holding the aircraft straight and level. It was a real test of strength too as you could see the red neck on the student in front of you as they pumped the gear down with 18 back and forth movements on the lever to get the gear fully down. At 17½ pumps you would be really struggling to get that last green light on the gear. To add to the mix, power was always required towards the end of the pumping cycle, another hand swapping requirement! We landed without flaps when practicing hydraulic failures as in reality you wouldn't be able to deploy them if hydraulics failed".

The Periscope

Unlike more modern tandem seat military trainers, the Fouga did not have stepped seating to allow the instructor in the rear cockpit to have an unobstructed forward view over the head of the student pilot in the front seat. Instead the Fouga was fitted with a large periscope, an optical instrument more commonly associated with submarines, through which the instructor was provided with a

forward view. Some instructors liked it and some didn't. As Paul recalls,

"If you chose not to use the periscope you became pretty adept at landing the aircraft by looking past the shoulders of the student or looking out the side and judging your height above the runway".

Later on, as an instructor on the Fouga, Paul was conscious of what could catch out the novice pilot:

"Obviously the speed was an issue and you just had to be careful not to exceed VNE. The 'g' characteristics of the aircraft was also an issue in that you could pull up to 5.8g on the Fouga officially but it was easy to accidentally pull up to 6g and even 6.5g. You just had to be careful not to do so. All this was done without a G-suit. You built up a tolerance for it. Once you knew what was coming, you were able to tense up your stomach muscles, thereby restricting the blood flow to your lower torso and avoiding

The instructors view from the back seat. Note the prominent periscope, a feature almost unique to the Fouga.
[Air Corps Photo Section]

a blackout. Though I remember one time coming back to Baldonnel, with Graeme Martin flying in the front cockpit and me in the back. We were holding over Kill, Co. Kildare when we got an unexpected but welcome clearance to come back to the field. Without warning he put the aircraft on its side and pulled us around. He couldn't see me in the rear cockpit but he called "Paul, are you OK? Are you all right back there?" But there was no response because I had passed out. His response to this was to lock his feet onto both rudder pedals and hold the controls firmly because the danger was that when a person starts to recover consciousness they do what we call the 'funky chicken', involuntary movements and twitching as blood returns to the upper torso and head and consciousness is regained, which because of the small confines of the Fouga cockpit could result in accidental inputs to the controls. It only lasted a few seconds before I recovered.

On the Fouga in the aerobatic scenario there was no torque from a propeller to contend with coming from a single propeller on say the Marchetti. Aerobatics on the Fouga were nice and smooth. If you wanted to do a loop you just pulled the stick back to 4g and let her come around, easing off the 'g' over the top, and reapplying in the pull out. You didn't need to put in any rudder or anything like that. Overall it was easier to fly aerobatics in the Fouga than in the Marchetti".

Weapons Training

For weapons training, the Fouga was armed with two 7.62mm machine guns in the nose and two Matra six-round pods containing 68mm SNEB rockets. As Paul recounts:

"Really the whole scenario was about safety. As you approached the armed aircraft there were two extra streamers [remove before flight tags] on the aircraft which were only removed once the canopy was

down, engines started and we were pointed away from buildings and personnel. These were the safety pins on the arming mechanisms for the rocket pods. After that it was standard stuff, we took the aircraft up to Gormanston which was a coastal Air Station (now closed) around the Dublin Control Area. Targets were placed approximately 300m off the shore line. We flew the firing circuit at 3000 feet, came in on base leg and literally did a wingover and put to put the nose down onto the target. You had to have your sights on the target during that initial nose down. If you had to make any adjustments after that you weren't at the races, you wouldn't be putting rounds anywhere near the target.

Notwithstanding the earlier problems experienced with the guns, by this time [1990's] the guns were very reliable, certainly when compared to the rockets. Sure, you would get stoppages from time to time but by and large you would be able to empty at least one of the guns onto the target. However, with the rockets it was a different story. The wiring was so old and we only did rocket practice once a year so the electrical connections were not as good as they ought to have been. It was not unusual to come back with three of the six rockets still in the pod. On one occasion when I fired the rockets all six rockets in one pod fired but none of the rockets on the other side left the pod! If returning with live ordnance there would be a crew waiting for us on the taxiway to disarm the weapons and make them safe."

Spinning the Fouga

Spin training is an essential part of any aircraft handling course but the Fouga had unique peculiarities in this respect due to the V-tail configuration. As John Mulvanny explains:

"The Fouga was a docile aircraft and very nice to fly but it had one vice, spinning. The V-tail was essentially a combined elevator and rudder, called a ruddervator, the two separate controls that are needed for spin recovery. The spin rate was relatively docile in the deliberately entered spin, but if you mishandle the spin recovery it could develop into a fast spin, where you went from a rotation every three to four seconds to one of at least twice that rate. There had been a number of Fouga accidents in other air forces as a result of spinning. As I reflect back to my 50 hours on the Fouga as a cadet, I think most of us were almost terrified of getting into a spin, but later on, during the operational course and when we began instructing on type, John Kelly and I, with more confidence in the aircraft and in ourselves, began deliberately getting ourselves into fast spins to figure out the best instructional method to teach people how to recover from them. Initially a spin was taught by applying the spin entry actions,

Fouga 217 being craned onto a truck following its forced landing near Whitegate Oil Refinery in Cork. The pilot did well to put it down intact on a grass field. This was the first occasion on which the wings were removed from a Fouga by Air Corps personnel, a job usually carried out in France during major overhauls. [Sgt. Pat Cornally Photo]

completing two rotations and recover, but we found if you let the spin develop more, by holding the aircraft in the spin for three or four rotations, the student became more comfortable in that environment and could think through the recovery actions. Spin recovery on the Fouga was slightly different to normally configured aircraft, with rudder and stick input movements separate because of the ruddervator. It involved first, the application of opposite rudder and then 2 seconds later moving the stick to neutral or slightly forward of neutral to unstall the aircraft. Mixing up of these recovery actions could lead to the fast spin, which could only be recovered from by reapplying normal spin actions and attempting the recovery actions once again. We never taught fast spins with students, but we did teach these corrective actions should they find themselves in such a situation. We would generally enter spins from 20,000 feet, do three rotations and recovery, losing about 8,000 feet of altitude while doing so".

To illustrate why spinning in a Fouga was approached with a great deal of caution, Brigadier General Paul Fry recalls an incident from early on in his flying career:

"Myles Cassidy and myself got into an inverted spin during my 50-hour handling check in 1976, when during the recovery after a three-turn spin I pushed the stick too far forward (and probably too briskly!) with the result that we flipped over the top onto our back! Taken by surprise at this development I left the opposite rudder applied and she remained inverted flicking into a spin immediately. Round we went and I just sat there trying to figure out what to do next - and all the time losing altitude at a quick rate. Myles took it from me and applied the correct recovery action - opposite rudder, stick BACK to beyond neutral, pause - two - three - centralise everything as soon as the spin stopped, which it did. We 'pulled through' from the inverted glide that we recovered into, passing through 8000 feet on the way to a zoom-climb and rolling-off-top of the loop. We had started the first spin at 18000 feet so we had used up a great deal of altitude. Myles gave the aircraft back to me and we climbed back up and repeated the exercise, without the inverted bit, of course. The next time I experienced an inverted spin was in the Super Tucano in 2002, and this time it was by way of a deliberate entry"!

Incidents and near misses

The Fouga was well liked by pilots and had an excellent safety record with the Air Corps. Nevertheless, there were a few occasions where the aircraft gave their pilots some heart-stopping moments. Both Commandant Geoffrey O'Byrne-White and Commandant Myles Cassidy

experienced double engine flameouts during takeoffs from very wet runways. This was due to the low slung intakes ingesting water splashed up from the nose wheel. On another occasion Captain Graeme Martin recalled flying as No. 2 in a three-ship formation led by Captain Martin Duffy at one of the Salthill Air shows at Galway when the No. 3 flown by Captain Paddy McNamee suffered an engine failure at the top of a loop. He had to break away and make an emergency landing.

On another occasion Commandant Myles Cassidy experienced a bird strike while flying the Fouga, the unfortunate bird having struck the wing in the vicinity of the airbrakes resulting in these being jammed in the open position. Commandant Cassidy made an emergency landing but the damage to the airbrakes was substantial enough to necessitate a lengthy repair.

On 24 April 1991 potentially the most serious incident involving a Fouga occurred when Lieutenant John Finn was forced to make an emergency landing in a large field near the Whitegate Oil Refinery in Co. Cork as a result of fuel starvation. Fortunately no serious damage occurred to either aircraft or pilot and the Fouga was recovered by truck the following day and brought back to Baldonnel.

Another incident occurred during a low-level flight by two Fougas over forestry near Nenagh Co. Tipperary when the No. 2 aircraft experienced severe vibration. The pilot immediately climbed to altitude and after a quick scan of the instruments could find nothing amiss. Following an emergency landing at Shannon, the fault was soon spotted. During some high 'g' manoeuvring the two air deflectors mounted on both sides of the front canopy frame had deployed. These are designed to create turbulent airflow in the event that the canopies are jettisoned during an emergency, thus aiding the egress of the pilots. On this occasion the wire that usually holds the air deflectors in the closed position had failed unexpectedly, resulting in the vibration experienced by the crew.

There were some lighter moments as well. Pilots wore parachutes that were connected to the seat harness via a D-ring on the left shoulder strap. It was not uncommon for a weary trainee pilot to forget to disconnect the static line from the seat harness prior to exiting the aircraft only to have the parachute deploy as the pilot walked away from the jet and reached the full extent of the static line, much to the amusement of anyone watching nearby.

Map showing the low-level flying training route designed by Commandant John Flanagan through the Dublin Wicklow Mountains. [Map reproduced by courtesy of Barry Dalby of EastWest Mapping]

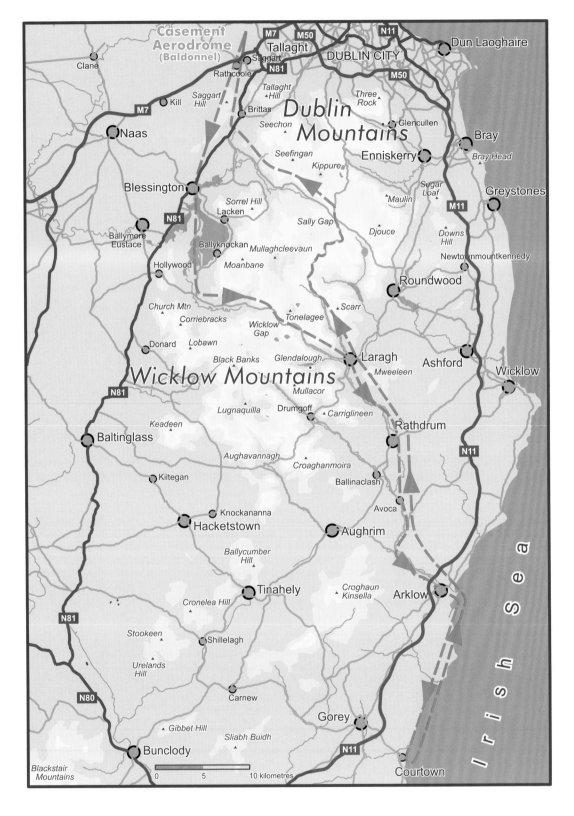

Chapter 5

The Silver Swallows Story

Above: The Silver Swallows practise their routine over Baldonnel.
[Air Corps Photo Section]

Early Days

By the early 1980s, many of the difficulties encountered with the initial service entry of the Fouga had been overcome and a steady pattern developed of annual flying training courses and military exercises in which the Fouga participated. The Fouga also appeared at air shows throughout the country. The premier Irish air shows during that period were the 'Air Spectaculars' held annually at Fairyhouse racecourse near Dublin, but which later moved to Baldonnel and other venues. The 1981 Air Spectacular featured a flyby of four Fougas led by Captain Geoffrey O'Byrne-White accompanied by Lieutenant Con Murphy, Lieutenant Tony Regan and Lieutenant Dermot McCarthy. No vertical formation manoeuvres were carried out during this display. While solo aerobatics had always been an integral part of military flying in Ireland, formation aerobatics

The 'Diamond' was the basic formation maintained throughout the initial stages of the display. [Air Corps Photo Section]

were not carried out, at least not officially; however, away from public gaze on training details over the midlands some pilots managed to incorporate formation aerobatics into their training. As Geoffrey O'Byrne White recalls;

"We had carried out a formation flypast at the Air Spectacular at Fairyhouse Racecourse on 16 August 1981 but this was just a flypast, there were no vertical manoeuvres during the display. I had completed conversion training on the BAE 125-700, but if not scheduled to fly that aircraft I kept my flying skills up to date by flying details on the Fouga. It was during one of these details on 8 October 1981 that my first formation loop with another Fouga Magister was carried out by myself and Captain Con Murphy in the company of reserve officer Tom Murphy (reserve officers were former Air Corps pilots who maintained their reserve status by attending two weeks of military service each year). As an aside it was around the same time we also carried out the first touch and go landing by a jet aircraft at Sligo's then new airport at Strandhill. From then on, every time the opportunity arose we ensured that formation aerobatics were included in the training details. I was Operations Officer and second-in-command of No.1 Support Wing at the time so I signed off on those details. It wasn't exactly a secret that we were carrying out formation aerobatics in the Fouga, though I'm not sure how much the senior Air Corps officers were actually aware of it".

1982 marked the 60th anniversary of the founding of the Air Corps and a special event to mark the occasion was planned at Baldonnel. The Fouga Magisters — led by Captain John Flanagan, Officer Commanding of the Light Strike Squadron — would be the highlight of the aerial activities, being scheduled to display in front of a select crowd of dignitaries and guests as John recalls;

"Over the years displays by Air Corps aircraft were relatively low key, consisting of a flyby followed by a formation change, then back in front of the crowd again and that was about it. I had it in mind that we would put on a proper show on this occasion, do something a little bit different from what had been done previously. I had three very good people on the team, Tony Regan, Dermot McCarthy and Nick McHugh. We sat down and designed a routine that would keep us tight to the airfield for most of the display (a feature of most Fouga displays from that time onward) but with a finale that would surprise the crowd. We went out and practised the routine over the Bog of Allen in the midlands and when the big day arrived the display went according to plan, consisting of a series of flybys with some rolls and formation changes. For the finale, we flew line abreast towards the hangars where the crowd was assembled, with me on the right, Dermot McCarthy on the far left and with Nick and Tony in the middle. On my command Dermot and I climbed up and commenced a 180 degree turn in opposite directions while the two lads in the middle accelerated straight ahead over the hangars before doing a U-turn to come back across the display line while myself and Dermot completed our turn through 270 degrees to do a crossover. This was timed so that we did the crossover just as the two lads would meet us in the middle of the display line but at 90 degrees to us. We all did a roll and disappeared from view before coming back in on finals. It looked pretty

spectacular. I remember afterwards being congratulated by J.J. Sullivan, a former Air Corps pilot who was then a senior captain flying Boeing 747s with Aer Lingus and who was also the display pilot for the Aer Lingus DH84 Dragon vintage biplane. He shook me by the hand and said 'Now that's what it's all about' and I went away thinking we could do more.

In January 1983 I was sent on the Command and Staff course at the Military College in the Curragh. I was promoted to Commandant while I was there and when I got back to Light Strike Squadron some months later I had a chat with Tony Regan about formation aerobatics in the Fouga. We were doing this ourselves. We had no terms of reference on which to draw. Although other air forces were using the Fouga as a mount for their aerobatic teams, notably France and Belgium, we hadn't any contact with them at the time so we really taught ourselves how to do formation aerobatics in the Fouga. Tony is a very capable pilot and we discussed the pros and cons of doing vertical manoeuvres in the Fouga, what power settings to use, the speeds at which we should enter the various parts of the routine and so on. Having discussed it at length, Tony finally said that the only way to test it was to try it. So off we went, out over the Bog of Allen, to practise these manoeuvres. When the two of us were comfortable in formation aerobatics, the most natural next step was to add a third aircraft. So I approached Dermot McCarthy, told him what we were doing and asked him if he would be interested in joining us to which he said yes. We continued practicing as a three-ship, initially at 15,000 feet to give us some margin for recovery in the event of a mishap, bringing it down gradually as we built up experience so that we could display in front of a crowd".

First Formation Loop at a Public Display

The 1983 'Air Spectacular' took place on Sunday 21 August at Fairyhouse, with a wide range of acts including a Lockheed C-141 Starlifter at one end of the size spectrum and the diminutive Wallis Autogyro 'Little Nellie' at the other. The Air Corps also provided a wide selection of aircraft that afternoon, including the BAe 125 Executive Jet, Beech Super Kingair, Gazelle and Alouette III helicopters and no less than two display teams; one team was made up of instructors from Basic Flying Training School flying the Marchetti and the other being the Fougas of Light Strike Squadron led by Commandant John Flanagan. The schedule for the day as initially proposed was for the Marchettis to display before the Fougas, but as John recalls there was a change in plan:

"We were supposed to display after the Marchettis. The weather wasn't too bad but it wasn't great either.

For what we were planning to do we didn't want any problems with the weather. As the Marchettis were about to commence their routine we were holding off behind the stands at Fairyhouse out of sight of the crowd when the cloud began to thin and we got a clear patch of blue sky over the display line. The Marchetti leader called me on the radio and asked if I wanted the sky to which I replied "you've read my mind" so we swapped timings and we went ahead with our display, which included the first formation loop ever to be carried out by Air Corps Fouga Magisters in front of an assembled crowd. That changed things considerably for the Air Corps and future aerobatic displays. The crowd loved it. We had proved that formation aerobatics could be done safely and we set a new target to aim for as far as future Air Corps display pilots were concerned. Things were never quite the same afterwards".

Somewhat surprisingly given their success in 1983, the following season did not feature a formation display by Fouga Magisters. As John Flanagan recalls:

"In 1984 we would have done it again but unfortunately as incoming Training School Commandant I was on Cadet interview boards all summer and Tony Regan was away doing other things. The General Officer Commanding, Brigadier General McMahon called me in and said that following the reaction to the 1983 Air Spectacular we should give the public more of the same. I pointed out that without the specific pilots being available to practise, it simply was not possible. I suggested a Singleton display, by Lieutenant Dermot McCarthy, who displayed at various air shows that summer".

New Personnel – New Routines

Commandant John Flanagan took over as officer commanding the Air Corps Flying Training School in 1984 and this left a gap in Light Strike Squadron that had to be filled. With the usual shuffling of personnel into various posts as promotions and retirements came into effect, Captain Kevin Barry was assigned the role of Chief Flying Instructor with Light Strike Squadron. He became the driving force behind the re-introduction of Fouga formation aerobatics in 1985. As Kevin describes it:

"Really, Light Strike Squadron was the de-facto advanced training school for the Air Corps. Our primary responsibility was to provide aircraft and instructors for the advanced flying phase of the annual 'Wings' course. So the whole idea was that we would work really hard to ensure that we would finish that course early in June to give the team members enough time to practise formation flying for the air show season.

The technicians were the unsung heroes of Light Strike Squadron. They were very professional and took

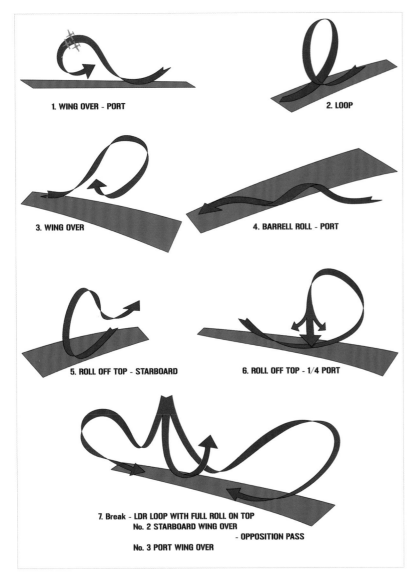

1. WING OVER - PORT

2. LOOP

3. WING OVER

4. BARRELL ROLL - PORT

5. ROLL OFF TOP - STARBOARD

6. ROLL OFF TOP - 1/4 PORT

7. Break - LDR LOOP WITH FULL ROLL ON TOP
No. 2 STARBOARD WING OVER
- OPPOSITION PASS
No. 3 PORT WING OVER

Schematic of the 1986 aerobatic display flown with these aircraft.

great pride in managing to keep at least four aircraft, and most often five aircraft, out of six serviceable at all times. As a small incentive or reward to the technical staff we undertook that we would send them on a one week summer camp with the Army if they could provide us with enough serviceable aircraft to finish the 'Wings' course early. The summer camp usually took place at an army barracks in either Lahinch in Co. Clare or Tralee in Co. Kerry. It involved the apprentices doing all sorts of things like hill walking, pot holing, sailing, rock climbing and all that sort of stuff. By the time we came back, which would have been around the end of June, we would then have had all of July to do the formation flying training. Throughout the summer we would also train a new instructor for the following year and that was the sequence of events over the five year period when I was with Light Strike Squadron".

For the 1985 season, the 'Air Spectacular' was moved from Fairyhouse to Cork Airport as part of the Cork 800 celebrations that were scheduled to take place in that city throughout the summer. Lieutenant

John Kelly and Lieutenant John Mulvanny were still in-situ as the only non–instructor pilots assigned to Light Strike Squadron at the time so it was a natural choice for Kevin Barry to select these two officers for the formation display team. John Mulvanny gives an account of his induction into formation display flying:

"Kevin Barry had to work hard to get us up to speed and we did a lot of formation practise with him, working up to steep inverted wingovers with smooth formation changes. As the day for the Cork show approached (18 August 1985) we were quite happy with wingovers but we hadn't quite gotten into looping or barrel rolling. This meant that the display would be relatively short but we were very young and very green. I remember being very happy with what we had planned on doing that year for Cork".

However, the weather was to wreak havoc with the air show that weekend forcing its cancellation. As John Mulvanny recalls:

"We flew down to Shannon on the day before the Cork show. Shannon is closer to Cork than Dublin and there was plenty of ramp space for visiting aircraft. The weather was terrible and we barely scraped into Shannon in very poor visibility. We parked up beside a German Navy F-104 Starfighter and a US Air Force F-16 and we thought we were in great company! The next day the weather was even worse. Regrettably the organisers had no option but to cancel the show".

In 1986, the Fouga display team members were once again Captain Kevin Barry as leader with Lieutenant John Mulvanny and Lieutenant John Kelly as wingmen. Practise started in June and by July the team were performing full loops. As Kevin Barry recalls:

"A special event had been planned for 26 July 1986 to celebrate the 50th anniversary of the Apprentice School at Baldonnel. That was when the first loop was done under my tenure as leader. The top brass were not aware that this was going to happen. The GOC called me into his office afterwards and asked me basically are we going to continue that (doing formation loops) and was I happy to continue to do so. I said yes, sure. That was it; tacit permission was given to continue formation aerobatics in the Fouga".

The annual 'Air Spectacular' air shows that had been held at Fairyhouse moved to Baldonnel for the first time in 1986, with the show taking place on 17 August. John Mulvanny remembers that particular display very well:

"It was an absolutely glorious day and there were massive crowds. As we flew overhead to commence our display, the sun glinted off a solid line of cars stretching all the way back to Rathcoole on the dual carriageway that runs close to Baldonnel. As this was our first full

aerobatic display with barrel rolls and loops, I really didn't want to mess it up in front of such a large crowd and on home turf as well! Thankfully, the display went very well and I remember being just relieved when I got to the 3-ship burst and positioned to land".

Although the team was in its second season of display flying they were still relatively inexperienced in the art of formation flying. It was as if each time a team of pilots was assembled they had to re-learn the techniques from scratch. John Mulvanny describes it thus:

"The Fouga's Marboré VI engine didn't have the quickest spool up time, so during aerobatic manoeuvres unless you anticipated the requirement for added power, it was too late and you had lost position in the formation. When we started doing barrel rolls for instance, we hadn't yet mastered a fool proof technique of how to maintain position in the formation, if you didn't anticipate the exact moment to add or remove power. We eventually learnt to overcome this problem by the knack of keeping the power on but maintaining your position with judicious use of the airbrake, the airbrake extending or retracting far quicker than the engine reacted to demands for power. Equally, if you started to get out of position in a loop, we learnt that the quickest way to correct this, without waiting for the power to come in, was to pull a little more G thus reducing the circumference of your loop relative to the leader. From the audience's point of view nobody would ever notice that you are doing this but we only learned this bit of technique in the second year. We rarely got it wrong but we still didn't have the experience that years of practise bring and it isn't easy to transfer this type of experience along from one generation to the next unless you have a sufficient cadre of pilots to talk to who have done it before".

Birth of the Silver Swallows

The 1987 display season brought a change in personnel as Lieutenant John Kelly and Lieutenant John Mulvanny were busy attending their own Instructors course that year. Captain Kevin Barry remained as team leader and he was joined by Captain Jack Killoch in the number two position with Lieutenant Pearse McCrann in the number three position. A new addition to the display that year was the introduction of a fourth aircraft, flown by Captain Tony Regan.

Training commenced for the summer display season during the spring of 1987, with much of this being carried out in the evenings and at weekends. Kevin Barry recalls adding a number of new manoeuvres to the display that year:

"We added a 'champagne break' or 'bomb burst',

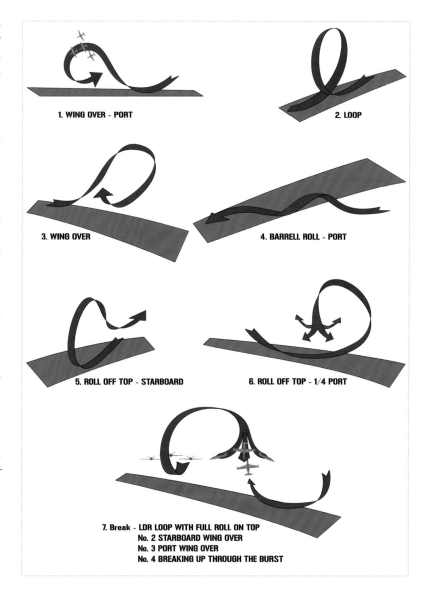

1. WING OVER - PORT

2. LOOP

3. WING OVER

4. BARRELL ROLL - PORT

5. ROLL OFF TOP - STARBOARD

6. ROLL OFF TOP - 1/4 PORT

7. Break - LDR LOOP WITH FULL ROLL ON TOP
No. 2 STARBOARD WING OVER
No. 3 PORT WING OVER
No. 4 BREAKING UP THROUGH THE BURST

with three of the aircraft diving vertically from altitude and splitting away in different directions. Captain Tony Regan flew a dynamic display as a singleton during part of the routine as the other three positioned for the 'champagne break'. This was in keeping with the principle of maintaining something interesting happening in front of the crowd at all times. Tony had to manoeuvre hard, pulling almost 6 'g' to get into position to zoom upwards into the centre of the break as the other three aircraft descended. We also introduced 'rollbacks' during that year. The 'rollbacks' were Jack Killoch's idea. These required the wingmen to perform two simultaneous full deflection rolls in opposite directions, which looked very effective when done well. They were technically in my opinion the most difficult and dangerous part of the display, completed in front of the crowd at 300 feet, a really great idea and show stopper by Jack Killoch.

We had three different routines worked out, the high, medium or low-level depending on the weather conditions prevailing at the time of our display. Naturally, we always wanted to do the high level one with full vertical

Schematic of the 1987 aerobatic display flown with 4 aircraft.

Right: The 'Mirror Pass' as seen from the crowd line.
[Paddy J. Cummins Photo]

Right: Viewed here from the rear seat of one Fouga is the other Fouga in the Mirror Pass. The upper Fouga is not trailing smoke. That's fuel from the vent pipe!
[Air Corps Photo Section]

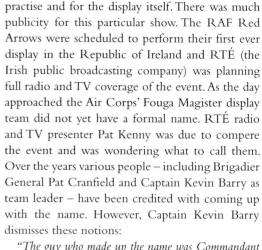

Below: The 1989 Silver Swallows Display Team. From L-R Lt. John Kelly No. 2, Lt. John Mulvanny No. 4, Capt. Kevin Barry (Team Leader) No. 1, Lt. John Hurley No. 3. This photo was taken outside the Light Strike Squadron building, the former Aer Lingus air terminal at Baldonnel dating from 1936!
[John Mulvanny Collection]

manoeuvres if the weather allowed. The low-level display was the hardest to fly because it required us to pull 6g a lot of the time to stay in front of the crowd".

The premier air display in Ireland that year was scheduled to take place at Baldonnel on Sunday 15 August and the technical staff worked hard all year to ensure that four aircraft would be available for

practise and for the display itself. There was much publicity for this particular show. The RAF Red Arrows were scheduled to perform their first ever display in the Republic of Ireland and RTÉ (the Irish public broadcasting company) was planning full radio and TV coverage of the event. As the day approached the Air Corps' Fouga Magister display team did not yet have a formal name. RTÉ radio and TV presenter Pat Kenny was due to compere the event and was wondering what to call them. Over the years various people – including Brigadier General Pat Cranfield and Captain Kevin Barry as team leader – have been credited with coming up with the name. However, Captain Kevin Barry dismisses these notions:

"The guy who made up the name was Commandant Ken Byrne who was Officer Commanding Flying Training Schools. He may have come up with it in conjunction with Captain Kevin Byrne (who was the public relations officer at the time.) I was too busy organising other things to think up a name for the team!"

Later that day when the four Fouga Magisters turned onto the runway, gleaming in their silver and dayglo red colours in the sunshine, Pat Kenny announced them to the crowd of over 100,000 spectators as the Irish Air Corps Silver Swallows aerobatic display team before handing over to Captain Kevin Byrne for the actual commentary. The name stuck and the Silver Swallows aerobatic display team was born.

The Silver Swallows continued to perform at various air shows over the next few years, with Captain Kevin Barry as team leader and occasional changes in personnel for the two wing and the number four positions. The aircraft and instructors were required for the Air Corps' various 'Wings' courses and operational commitments in support of the Army and Naval Service throughout the year, so the team reformed each spring with new members being coached through formation aerobatics with the team leader before joining the other members for full formation aerobatics approximately six to ten weeks before the display season got underway. Members of the Silver Swallows during the period 1986 to 1989 included Lieutenant John Mulvanny, Lieutenant John Kelly, Lieutenant Pearse McCrann, Lieutenant John Hurley, Captain Tony Regan and Captain Jack Killoch, with the aforementioned Captain Kevin Barry as team leader during that time.

'Air Spectacular 88' was held again at Baldonnel and once again the Silver Swallows performed an admirable display, albeit in very turbulent conditions. John Mulvanny remembers it as:

"A woeful day, a day that was incredibly windy and

turbulent. I think there was an Aer Arann Islander that flew backwards with the headwind; it was that kind of day. I had never flown an aircraft in formation in such turbulence, the aircraft was literally bucking around you and it's incredible when you see it on video afterwards, you can actually see each aircraft just bouncing around the place. The high wind obviously made Kevin's job more difficult from a positional point of view and the air was so lumpy, it meant you were working really hard to stay in formation".

The Silver Swallows were not the only Air Corps aircraft to perform aerobatics at that event. The current General Officer Commanding, Brigadier General Paul Fry, performed an extraordinary display of airmanship in the piston-engine SIAI Marchetti SF260W Warrior of Basic Flying Training School.

The 1989 team consisted of Captain Kevin Barry in the number one position, Lieutenant John Kelly back in the number two slot, Lieutenant John Hurley as number three and Lieutenant John Mulvanney as number four.

Each season brought new manoeuvres to the display routine. One such manoeuvre that looked spectacular from the crowd's point of view was the Mirror Pass with half roll. The standard 'Mirror Pass' required the leader to fly along the display line while the No. 4 rolled inverted and put the nose of his aircraft into the space between the 'V' tails of the leader's aircraft. For the 1989 season the team added a half roll to the Mirror formation midway along the display line which required the leader and No. 4 to roll while staying in the Mirror. This was a difficult manoeuvre as John Mulvanny describes it.

"I was doing the 'Mirror' in 1989 as number four and I rolled my aircraft inverted and fit into the 'V' tail of Kevin's aircraft. That bit I was totally comfortable with, but half way up the display line we both did a half roll but more often than not I would end up skewed out of line with Kevin's aircraft. I got that one right about once in four times during practise. Of all the manoeuvres that we carried out over the years that's the one I think we should not have put it into the display because I just didn't have it down to a level that it could be performed consistently well".

With each season the reputation of the team grew. It was not long before invitations were being received for the team to display at overseas events and in 1989 the Silver Swallows topped the bill at an air show in Newtonards Co. Down in Northern Ireland. This was a breakthrough for the Silver Swallows, performing outside the Republic of Ireland for the first time. It was also before the Northern Ireland peace process had been put in place so it was quite

an event for five Air Corps Fouga Magisters to turn up at Belfast's Aldergrove Airport!

Described as a force of nature by his colleagues, the early development of the Silver Swallows owes much to the leadership of Kevin Barry. Kevin had the skill level, the drive, the personality and the self-confidence to convince others that formation aerobatics in the Fouga could be done well and done safely. Looking back on his time as team leader, Kevin Barry describes the rationale behind setting up the team in the first place:

"Really, I just wanted to do it from the very beginning. I believe the Air Corps could have had a formation display team much earlier had there been a will to do so. We had the aircraft, we had talented pilots and we had talented technicians on the ground and when all these things come into line it was a case of let's do it. This was a once in a lifetime opportunity, you get out there and grab it because it wasn't going to happen otherwise.

There was an original Aer Lingus terminal at Baldonnel. We took it over as a headquarters for Light Strike Squadron, scrounging around the place for furniture to set up briefing rooms and so on. For me, 1985 and 1986 were proof of concept. After that I wanted it to be a fully fledged display team. Had we managed to display abroad a bit earlier we might have obtained some funding. We did very well in Ireland in 1987, 1988 and 1989. We performed a four-ship display for the opening of the new runway at Dublin Airport on 21 June 1989 with the then Taoiseach [i.e., the Irish Prime Minister], Charles J. Haughey in attendance. It was important to display in front him and to impress him. If he was impressed then the top brass had to take us seriously.

As the standing of the team grew amongst the public, it did wonders for Light Strike Squadron at Baldonnel. Once the whole thing kicked off everybody started to get

The 1990 Silver Swallows Team members from L-R, Lt. Kieran Friel, Lt. John Mulvanny (Team leader), Lt. Martin Duffy, Lt. John Kelly. This photo was taken at at RAF Brawdy, shortly before their first ever overseas display.
[Lt. Col. Kevin Byrne Photo]

Line up of participants at the 1990 Air Spectacular at Shannon Airport taken from the door of a Dauphin helicopter.
Visible in this photo are the Silver Swallows lined up with their Spanish and Italian counterparts, the Halciones and the Frecce Tricolori and an array of USAF aircraft.
[Lt. Col. Kevin Byrne Photo]

interested and everybody wanted to be in it (i.e., Light Strike Squadron). Whereas before, nobody wanted to be in the squadron because it was like death, you were nothing. Now you were getting more flying time, you were flying a jet and on top of that you were doing formation aerobatics. That's why people wanted to get into it. We wanted the best pilots to be instructors and it was an incentive to be an instructor if you knew you were going to be a member of the Silver Swallows as well. We also saw the benefit of using the Silver Swallows as a recruiting tool for the Air Corps and for showing off as a military organization that we can compete with the best."

Highlights of the 1990 Display Season

In 1990, the Silver Swallows received an invitation to perform an aerobatic display at RAF Brawdy in Wales. RAF Brawdy was home to a detachment of No. 202 Squadron, flying search and rescue Westland Sea King helicopters and a good rapport had been built up between this squadron and the Air Corps personnel of No. 3 Support Wing performing search and rescue duties with their Alouette IIIs. The then Tánaiste (i.e.,

the Irish Deputy Prime Minister) and Minister for Defence, Mr. Brian Lenehan accepted the invitation and the Air Corps set about planning for the event. Matters were complicated somewhat by the posting of Captain Kevin Barry away from Light Strike Squadron to take up a role with Maritime Squadron. Although he was no longer available to fly with the team he remained on as team manager, where he used his considerable organisational skills to ensure that all of the activities of the Silver Swallows would run smoothly. It was a tall order for the technical staff too. They would have to ensure that five out of the six Fouga Magisters would be serviceable so as to provide a spare aircraft for the four-ship formation in the event any of the aircraft had a technical problem that would render it unserviceable for a display.

The new team leader was Lieutenant John Mulvanny, who had previous experience with the Silver Swallows as a wingman. He was joined by Lieutenant John Kelly, also an experienced member of the Silver Swallows and two new members of the team with no previous formation aerobatic experience, Lieutenant Kieran Friel and Lieutenant

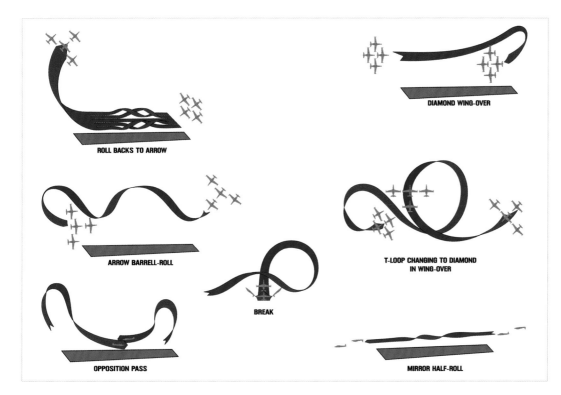

ROLL BACKS TO ARROW

DIAMOND WING-OVER

ARROW BARRELL-ROLL

T-LOOP CHANGING TO DIAMOND IN WING-OVER

BREAK

OPPOSITION PASS

MIRROR HALF-ROLL

Schematic of the 1990 display manoeuvres flown with four aircraft.

Martin Duffy. All had been classmates on the same 'Wings' course in 1984 and all had between 1500 and 1600 hours of flying time. With the date fast approaching for their first overseas display and with two new pilots to train up, the team was only given the opportunity to train on a full time basis from June, after the end of that year's 'Wings' course. It was a hectic time with the two primary air shows for the season, an Air Spectacular at Shannon and the display at RAF Brawdy scheduled to take place (earlier than previous years) within days of each other on 22 and 26 July respectively.

John Mulvanny remembers his time as team leader; "Kevin was going to Maritime Squadron and he basically said to me "you are it" and that was all there was to it. At any opportunity during the advanced stage of that year's wing course, I got some practise in with Kieran and Martin to bring them up to speed, so that when we got to full time training, it would be with the full formation. I remember for the 'Air Spectacular' at Shannon that the IAA wanted to vet us to ensure that

The Tornados break away from the Silver Swallows over Cork City and head back to Germany.
[Lt. Col. Kevin Byrne Photo]

our display was safe with respect to crowd safety and didn't break the display line but they did that to all the display teams. They had complained about our entry line on a few occasions but you wanted to make as much impact as possible and the best way of doing that was coming from behind the crowd. The Fouga is a small aircraft and we were not equipped with smoke which made us relatively difficult to pick up visually. So we were always trying to nibble away at the entry angle to come from behind the crowd line as much as possible. In 1990 every practise over Baldonnel was video-taped. It was the only way that I felt we were ever going to get feedback as to how to improve the display. It was a bit like improving your golf swing. You think you are doing okay but if you saw a video of it you would probably have corrected yourself. In fairness we had great support from photo section who carried out all the video recording and that helped a lot".

Although most of the practise flights took place in the environs of Baldonnel, the team took the opportunity to practise at Cork and Shannon

German Air Force Tornado tucked under the wing of the Fouga flown by John Mulvanny.
[John Mulvanny Collection]

47

The Light Strike Squadron technical team led by Flight Sergeant Des Higgins, who worked so hard to ensure five aircraft would be available for the first overseas display by the Silver Swallows, seen here at RAF Brawdy.

From Left to right:
Airman D. Ryan,
Airman J. Taylor,
Airman S. Pender,
Airman P. Doody,
Flight Sergeant D. Higgins,
Sergeant T. Crean,
Sergeant M. Bambrick,
Airman B. Doyle,
Corporal A. Campbell,
Corporal W. Whelan,
Airman J. Power,
Corporal P. Cornally,
Flight Sergeant J. Byrne,
Corporal D. Duane.
[John Mulvanny Collection]

airports to familiarise themselves with operating at different locations prior to the big show at Shannon on 22 July. The Shannon 'Air Spectacular' took place on a glorious Sunday afternoon with an excellent line up of foreign participants including the US Air Force with A-10 Thunderbolts, F-16 Fighting Falcons, F-4 Phantoms and a massive C-5 Galaxy transport. The German Air Force sent two Panavia Tornados, but the most interesting participants insofar as the Silver Swallows team members were concerned was the Italian Air Force, Frecce Tricolori display team operating Aermacchi MB339 jets and the Spanish Air Force display team, the Halciones operating CASA 101 Aviojets. The Silver Swallows would be performing in front of their peers in the relatively small world of military aerobatic teams. As John Mulvanny recalls:

"Personally I believe the Frecce Tricolori are the best at what they do. For the Shannon show our girlfriends had come down to watch the display. The Frecce had done their rehearsal before us and everyone had gone off to Nelly's bar for light refreshments. By the time we arrived after our own rehearsal the Frecce lads had our girlfriends surrounded in the bar! However, my most outstanding memory of that event is one of pride. We actually did display to a very professional level considering the lack of time we had and the resources that were given to us. Every single person in the squadron just worked their socks off in order to make it happen. I felt great pride in us all and privileged that I worked with a great bunch of pilots and technicians".

The provision of a spare aircraft was well founded when just hours before the display was due to take place one of the designated display Fougas developed an engine problem that looked like one of the pilots would have to switch to the spare aircraft. The technicians performed an engine change and

got spare parts flown down from Baldonnel. The display itself was performed without a hitch and everything was looking good for the trip to Brawdy the following week.

Tornado Formation

The day after the Shannon 'Air Spectacular', the Silver Swallows were scheduled to perform a display in Cork in honour of the first port call to that city by the passenger liner Queen Elizabeth II, better known simply as the QE2. Having gotten to know their German counterparts flying the two Tornado jets over the previous two days, a most unique and unofficial formation could be seen over Co. Kerry and Co. Cork that day. Following the Frecce Tricolori accident at an air show at

The T-Loop, a new manoeuvre for the 1990 Display season.
[Air Corps Photo Section]

The Air Corps Fouga Magisters at RAF Brawdy as seen from the Control Tower. Note the RAF Rescue Sea King helicopter in the background. [Lt. Col. Kevin Byrne Photo]

Ramstein a few years previously, Luftwaffe aircraft were banned from flying in formation with other air forces without prior authorisation. The German Tornadoes were on their way back to Germany and the Silver Swallows were on their way from Shannon to Cork so it was fortuitous that they 'just happened' to be flying in the same patch of sky for a few minutes before the Tornados broke off and headed for home.

First Overseas Display – RAF Brawdy

On Wednesday 26 July 1990 the five Fouga Magisters accompanied by a Beech Super Kingair carrying support staff and senior officers flew across the Irish Sea to RAF Brawdy. All personnel were accommodated on the base and the aircraft were parked overnight on the ramp just beside the control tower. The next morning one of the aircraft had developed a fault and it was proving impossible to start its engines. As Sergeant Pat Cornally recalls:

"The aircraft had been parked out overnight and we hadn't brought canopy covers with us. Normally this wouldn't be a problem as the aircraft are hangared each evening at Baldonnel, but during the night of 25 August it had rained heavily at Brawdy and some moisture had seeped into the cockpit of the aircraft in question. The moisture had trickled down the inside walls of the cockpit and was causing an electrical short which was preventing engine start up. If we didn't get this dried out before show time we were going to have a major problem. I remembered that one of the other techs had brought a hair dryer with him! I ran back to the accommodation block and told him I needed his hair dryer as a matter of urgency. He thought I was taking the mick but he handed over the hair dryer when he saw the look on my face. Equipped with the hair dryer and a long extension

lead I managed to get the electrics dried out and the engines started fine".

John Mulvanny describes the trip to Brawdy:

"The early nineties was still pre-peace process in Northern Ireland and I wondered how we would be received when we landed at Brawdy in Wales, but the people we met were all incredibly supportive, nice and friendly the exact same as ourselves. It is amazing how as military pilots we are all the same and they made us feel really at home. For our rehearsal I loosened the formation out a bit and took the team up and down the display line two or three times, to get everyone oriented to the landmarks around the airfield. It was easy enough for me as leader to keep track of our orientation to the display line during the routine, but for the wingmen it can be difficult to orientate themselves when they break away at low level if they are not familiar with the local landmarks. We also wanted to make sure that there were no aerials or other obstacles at low level that might interfere with our routine. After checking out the area for a few minutes we then commenced our display

Left: various stickers used as promotional giveaways by the Silver Swallows. The basic motif of the green white and orange arrow heads was designed by John Mulvanny in conjunction with his late father Jim Mulvanny.

Captain Peter McDonnell in 215 keeps an eye on formation leader Captain Graeme Martin in 220 as they take off for their first display at RAF Fairford in 1997.
[Peter Hopkins Photo]

routine rehearsal. When we landed one of the locals told us that he thought our initial runs up and down the display line was our actual display for the show but he was subsequently quite impressed when we actually did our stuff"!

A new manoeuvre for the 1990 season and one which was performed during the Brawdy display was the 'T Loop' in which three aircraft form up line abreast with the No. 4 directly behind the team leader. Other manoeuvres were rehearsed during the run up to the display season but were not ultimately included in the final routine. As John Mulvanny explains, one of these was the 'Card Loop':

"We had practised the card loop in which the four aircraft formed a perfect rectangle while executing the loop, the two front aircraft in line abreast with the other two directly behind. It wasn't all that effective if you saw it from the side but it was very effective if you did the card loop flying straight towards the crowd. In the end we decided not to incorporate it in the routine, not that we couldn't do it but because it would have required a fair bit of repositioning and also produced the problem of possibly breaking the display line. It would have looked great but we just couldn't incorporate it into the time scale of an 8.5 minute routine.

The standard formation that was used for early part of the sequence was the 'Diamond Four'. The tip tanks of the two wingmen's aircraft should line up directly behind

the left and right tip tanks of the leader respectively. In our 1990 routine the wing men would maintain the 'Diamond Formation' by lining up the pilot's head in the lead aircraft with the filler cap on his tip tank which was slightly behind centre. Then following behind, the No. 4 should also have his tip tanks lined up directly behind the leader. The No. 4 would always be offset slightly below the leader to avoid the jet wash from the lead aircraft's engines".

The Irish Air Corps first ever aerobatic display abroad commenced at 16:15 on Thursday 26 July 1990 and was very well received by the assembled crowd. The Silver Swallows were in good company, the RAF Red Arrows, the Italian Frecce Tricolori and the Dutch Grasshoppers Display team flying Alouette III's all performed at the Brawdy show. It was one of many occasions at which the Silver Swallows would share ramp space with some of the best display teams in the world.

Change in Tempo

Following the highly successful 1990 season, during which the Silver Swallows had achieved much of what they had set out to do in terms of gaining international recognition for the high standards of the Air Corps, acting as a recruitment vehicle to

attract young people to the Defence Forces and attracting the best Air Corps pilots to the instructor role, the period from 1991 to 1995 brought a reduction in tempo for the Silver Swallows. Flying displays continued but were fewer in number. The aircraft were getting old and the provision of spare parts was becoming problematic. In 1991 three of the aircraft had undergone 600 hour inspections, 215 and 220 in France and 216 at Baldonnel. As these were lengthy procedures taking up to four months and involving the complete disassembly of the aircraft this limited their availability for flight operations. In fact the total flying time for the six Fouga Magisters was just 511 hours that year. An invitation for the team to perform at the Royal International Air Tattoo at RAF Fairford in July was regretfully declined due to a shortage of available aircraft. However, a return visit to RAF Brawdy was made by a solitary Fouga (220) when that airfield hosted an air show on 25 July 1991. The late start to the 1992 'Wings' course meant that there was insufficient time for the team to train for the summer display season and no formation displays were performed that year.

Nevertheless, efforts were made to ensure that the team spirit and high morale of the Light Strike Squadron would continue in spite of these difficulties. Silver Swallows patches were designed and worn by team members. There was no shortage of enthusiasm to continue display flying but the lack of availability of aircraft was a source of frustration to many in Light Strike Squadron. The Silver Swallows were back in the air performing at the Air Spectacular on 11 July 1993 and at other displays throughout the country. In the normal course of events there were several changes to the team line-up during this period as personnel moved to other duties and with promotions and retirements. Captain Martin Duffy was team leader with Lieutenant Graeme Martin and Lieutenant Paddy McNamee respectively flying as numbers two and three. This trio flew a number of displays in the 1993-95 timeframe.

Silver Swallows Final Incarnation, 1996 – 1997

By 1996, newly promoted Captain Graeme Martin was the team leader and was keen that the Silver Swallows should recommence an extensive season of display flying. As Graeme recalls:

"I flew display formations for a few years in the number two position, starboard side. I also flew as the de-facto leader for some minor displays, as I was the Chief Flying Instructor in Light Strike Squadron. In 1996

we flew a number of short displays. By then I was team leader. Most notable was a display at Dun Laoghaire harbour over the USS John F Kennedy. There was a massive crowd gathered to see the aircraft carrier which was on a courtesy visit to Ireland. I asked permission from Colonel John O'Brien if he would authorize a display. He agreed. We arrived as a three-ship formation, completed a few very steep wing overs (inverted) and then I broke away and flew the solo display that I was authorized for. This way we could at least keep the idea of formation aerobatic displays alive. Interestingly I heard the day after the display that most observers assumed that we were the US Navy! The other two pilots for that one were number two Lieutenant Ronan Verling and number three Lieutenant Paul Whelan."

Paul Whelan's abiding memory following that display was of being invited on board the carrier and being given the opportunity to experience a catapult launch from the co-pilot's seat in an E-2C Hawkeye. The launch was a tremendous experience but the planned arrested landing back on the carrier did not come to pass as the USS John F. Kennedy steamed into a fog bank in the Irish Sea necessitating a diversion by the Hawkeye to the Fleet Air Arm Base at Yeovilton!

Towards the end of 1996 the writing was on the wall for the Fouga, with the Air Corps finding it increasingly difficult to source spare parts. In some instances the Air Corps found themselves in the position of having to barter with other air arms that had access to stocks of parts including consumables such as oil filters and tyres. Indeed, a replacement periscope for one of the aircraft was obtained from the Cameroon Air Force. It was a testament to the skills of the technical staff that they were able to keep four aircraft available out of six and on rare occasions even five out of six were available for flight training. Notwithstanding the difficulties of

Above: The 1997 Silver Swallows Team. From L-R Captain Graeme Martin (Team Leader), Captain Peter McDonnell, No. 2, Lieutenant Paul Whelan, No. 3 and Lieutenant Christian Keegan No. 4. [Comdt. Dave Corcoran Photo]

Above: For overseas displays during the 1997 season, the team leader's aircraft, Fouga 220, was fitted with a satellite navigation system. The GPS display was mounted in the front cockpit in the position usually occupied by the gunsight. The GPS antenna was mounted on the upper rear fuselage.
[John McFarland Photo]

maintaining these aircraft as the decade progressed, it was a very busy period for the Advanced Training School and it was also during this period that the Fouga was to gain considerable public acclaim with the reforming of the Silver Swallows display team as a four-ship formation.

Commandant Paul Whelan flew the number three position in the 1997 Silver Swallows team and he recounted their formation and work-up during an eight month period in 1996–1997:

"In 1996 it was recognised that the Fougas would not remain in service for more than about two more years given the hours that were on them and the difficulties in obtaining parts. 1997 was also the 75th Anniversary of the foundation of the Air Corps so with that in mind and the Fougas nearing the end of their service lives, Captain Graeme Martin approached the then General Officer Commanding, Brigadier General Pat Cranfield suggesting a season of Silver Swallows displays. The suggestion was agreed to with a heart and a half by the GOC and we began flying training. We were running 'Wings' courses at the same time so it was a very busy time with practises taking place in the evening and at weekends."

Captain Graeme Martin was the team leader; Captain Peter McDonnell was in the number two position to the right of the leader, with then Lieutenant Paul Whelan as number three on the left and Lieutenant Christian Keegan flying the number four position directly behind the leader.

Captain Martin was responsible for training the other pilots in the formation. In the words of Commandant Whelan:

"We started with baby steps, each of us would go out separately on a detail with Graeme Martin as a two-ship formation. We would practise formation flying starting with rate one turns then gradually increasing the rate of roll and angle of bank until we were comfortable doing this with only a few feet separating our aircraft. Then we would fly three to four details of high wingovers gradually moving on to full vertical manoeuvres. Graeme would do this with each of us in our various positions until we were proficient at full vertical loops.

Graeme decided from the very beginning not to fly in a very close formation. We would not fly in a loose formation either but in a strict 'distance apart' formation. The reason for that was that the spectators would be able to see the individual aircraft clearly from the ground. When the aircraft are in a tight, close formation the spectators can't easily distinguish one aircraft from another. So with our display routine the crowd get a much better profile of a four-ship display. However, that brings its own difficulties with the crowd being able to discern misalignments more easily in a Fouga formation with their long slender wings than say a formation of aircraft with delta wings where you can't easily distinguish the small discrepancies in position. So we had to adopt a very rigid and clinical approach to station keeping. My reference points for formating on the other aircraft were the pilot's head and the prominent aileron mass balance on the lead Fouga. By lining up the two I could keep the same relative position between the aircraft throughout the display. If I couldn't see the pilot's head it meant I had dropped slightly too low and could reposition upwards. With practise, the distance keeping became second nature and you became much more comfortable in the cockpit, much more capable of carrying out the routine checks required of any flight while still precisely 'in station'.

At the start of the workup there was a lot of 'white knuckle' flying. You were concentrating so hard because it was all new that you tended to grip the control column very tightly and were probably over-controlling to a certain degree. But after a while you realised that the same thermals that were affecting your leader were also affecting your aircraft in the same way. You could relax the grip a bit and the tenseness was gone. The spectators wouldn't see the effect on the formation because all of the aircraft in the formation were affected by thermals and turbulence in the same way.

We had the advantage of not being a very fast aircraft like the Alpha Jet or Hawk so Graeme designed the routine to keep the aircraft in front of the crowd throughout most of the display. This was exemplified by the start of the display where we performed two vertical loops one after the other at crowd centre followed by a high wing over and a port barrel roll. The barrel roll was one of those manoeuvres that could go wrong – not

in a dangerous sense but you could lose a man out of formation. Hand on heart it was probably the hardest manoeuvre for me to accomplish being on the outside of the formation barrel roll. You entered it at high speed and high g, pulling about 4g and by the time we were on the top of the roll I was having to push a little bit of negative g to stay in formation and use airbrakes to prevent my aircraft encroaching on the leader, before bringing on the power and the g once more in the recovery. It became routine after a while but it was one of the manoeuvres that could potentially put the formation out of alignment.

Then we went into a series of manoeuvres including high wingovers, line astern and the 'Arrowhead' with me and the other wingman, Peter McDonnell performing two simultaneous opposite sense rolls ('Rollbacks') that put us behind the number four. This was one of those manoeuvres that can't be performed by numbers in that you can't say you should enter it at 'such and such' a speed, pull 2g and roll left and right respectively. To get this to work, myself and Peter would go have a coffee and literally go through the movements ourselves watching our hands and how far they come back. We watched how the other entered a roll and we got a feel for how each of us was doing it. In essence we learned to synchronise our movements. On the ground one of us would sit in the cockpit while the other watched and again we practised putting in the same amount of control inputs at the same rate before practicing it in the air. We had to work a fair bit together and we remain great friends to this day.

We also performed the 'Opposition Pass'. Basically Peter would take a line, a definite reference on the ground, be it a runway, taxiway or some other straight-line feature. He would rigidly hold a height and speed as we flew towards each other from opposite directions. It's fairly obvious, but it was my job to miss him, just. From the crowd's perspective it looked like we were flying

Paddy the Pig! Adopted as an unofficial mascot for the 1997 display season, this cuddly toy was a great hit with the public when the aircraft were on static display at air shows at home and abroad. [Sgt. Pat Cornally Photo]

Paddy the Pig drew crowds of bystanders to view the Silver Swallows when they were parked up at airshows between display routines. Usually travelling in style in the supporting Beech Super Kingair, Paddy literally had the stuffing taken out of him so that he could travel back from the UK in the back seat of a Fouga! He turned up in all sorts of places in Baldonnel over the years! [Sgt. Pat Cornally Photo]

straight at each other but in fact I was slightly above and offset from him, quite close to him in fact, but as we passed each other, wing over wing at a closing speed of 600kts it looked quite spectacular from the ground.

Graeme and Chris would fly another manoeuvre called the 'Mirror Pass'. Chris would fly straight and level with Graeme flying inverted above him. That was hard work for Graeme because he had to roll upside down and push to remain in formation.

Fouga 217 brakes hard at the end of the team's first display at RAF Fairford in 1997. [Peter Hopkins Photo]

Captain Graeme Martin turns in for landing following the team's successful display at Fairford for which they were awarded the Lockheed Martin Cannestra trophy. Note the deployed airbrakes and flaps. [Peter Terlouw Photo]

We had a low-level routine in the event that there was a low cloud ceiling at the display venue. We had to perform this sequence at one of our overseas displays at Florennes in Belgium as there was a low ceiling that day. It certainly wasn't as exciting as the high-level routine, but if conditions changed we had the luxury of being able to change the sequence mid-routine if Graeme decided to do so. We had flown together so often that we were really quite comfortable doing this.

We had specific aircraft for each position in the formation based on the power available. Because of their age and general condition, though they were extremely well maintained, each aircraft had a slightly different power output. Generally the leader, Graham, would fly in 220 because it had a stable power output. I flew in 218 because it had a little bit of extra power available, particularly when you needed it at the top of the barrel roll. Peter, the other wingman, flew 216 on the right and Chris flew 217 in the number four position.

A minor incident occurred at the end of a practise session during the work up period. We were heading back to Baldonnel after training over the midlands when I thought I could smell smoke in the cockpit. We were at about 2000 feet and we were busy 'keeping station' on the leader so we generally had eyes on him. We didn't tend to look around

so I asked Graeme over the radio if we had flown through smoke. Sometimes we would fly through smoke if a farmer was burning stubble in the fields or if there was a gorse fire somewhere. Graeme said that we hadn't and I opened the vent to get rid of the smell. There didn't appear to be anything obviously wrong with the aircraft. We planned to do some more practise over the airfield so we climbed to altitude to get enough height to do the first loop and just as we got to the top of the loop I heard a bang from the rear cockpit and then I got a definite smell of acrid smoke that seemed like something electrical was burning. I just peeled off the formation and I made a 'pan-pan' call on the radio to Baldonnel and immediately headed back and made an emergency landing on runway 23. The fire guys were down the runway in the blink of any eye and they were extremely enthusiastic about dowsing 218 in foam which would have scuppered our display season. After shutting down on the runway it was all I could do to prevent them from killing 218 with foam and I remember shouting 'No No No, it's only electrical!' Fortunately it was only a transistor that had burned out and 218 was soon back in the air".

International Outings

A full programme of flying displays was planned for the 1997 season and there were plenty of overseas

invitations for the team in what was likely to be the last full year in which the Silver Swallows would operate. The team was scheduled to display on three separate occasions in the UK, 21 June at RAF Woodford, 19-20 July at RAF Fairford and 13 September at RAF Leuchars in Scotland. There was also a display planned for 6-7 September at Florennes in Belgium.

The first hurdle to be overcome was to gain written permission to display at air shows throughout the UK from the British authorities. As Graeme recalls:

"RAF Woodford was also a big event for us in 1997, as it was for this display that the UK Civil Aviation Authority and RAF informed us that they would send down an 'examining panel' to watch our display, and if we were good enough, they would give us written permission to display in the UK for the rest of the season. I think this became a requirement after a display team had a fatal crash at an airshow in Belgium. Therefore on the rehearsal day, we were being judged. So I submitted the display sequence, weather minimums etc. One was a good high level one, the second was a shorter flat display (for poor weather), not as spectacular to watch, but in some ways more difficult to fly. As it turned out, the weather was terrible. Rain, strong winds, low cloud base. We departed for our rehearsal, and there was just enough room (3,000 feet) to commence the high level display. All went well for the first vertical manoeuvres, but then the rain rolled in with a lower cloud base so I abandoned the display about 30 per cent in. I asked ATC if we could do our flat display, time was very tight, but they allowed us. In very difficult conditions (rain and cross wind) we completed about 80 per cent of the flat display, but again I abandoned the routine as the conditions were going below our planned minimums. We landed (the landing was described as formation aquaplaning by Peter McDonnell) and were a little disappointed as we had wanted to show the judging panel what we were capable of. Later that day I was introduced to the head of the judging panel who informed us that they were very impressed with our display, and were very confident in issuing us our display authorization. Obviously I was delighted, it's a shame that I don't have a copy of it, as I can clearly remember the A4 paper!

Unfortunately the following day the weather was also terrible. I can remember being in the control tower with the other team leaders, and solo display pilots. The organizers were keen for us all to fly. I can understand this as all that planning seems like a waste, when no one flies. However I remember double-checking the actual conditions, and determined that it was too poor, even for the flat display. I must admit I did feel bad, as I really wanted to fly. I remember the Red Arrows leader saying that they would get airborne and see what they could do. This made me feel even worse. However when they got

airborne they flew straight into the low cloud base and had to make an IFR recovery. I did bring this up over a beer that night with the leader who was a great guy, a little embarrassed, I learned a lot that day!"

Home Displays

One of the highlights of the 1997 display season was the Air Corps 75th Anniversary Families' Day that took place on 6 July 1997. Paul Whelan remembers that event:

"We had to perform the low-level display because the weather on the day at Baldonnel was overcast. That afternoon, however, we flew to Co. Galway in glorious weather to perform at the annual Salthill Air Show. Incidentally, it's infinitely more difficult to perform aerobatics over the sea than over land because you have no horizon and no external cues. It's like being in a goldfish bowl and you're taking your cues from the G forces you are experiencing rather than from what you can see peripherally outside.

Based on the original No. 1 Fighter Squadron badge from the 1940s, this Light strike Squadron badge was applied to the port side of the Fouga fuselage for the 1997 display season.

A new Silver Swallows badge was applied to the starboard side of the aircraft for the 1997 season.

Above: Taken moments after the team was awarded the Lockheed Martin Cannestra Trophy for the best flying display by an overseas participant, the delight on their faces is obvious to all.
[Graeme Martin Collection]

After the display we landed at Galway's Oranmore Airport to refuel and headed back to Baldonnel that evening. As it was a families' day there were still plenty of crowds at Baldonnel and by the time we got back the weather was excellent so we requested permission from the tower to do the display once more. Permission was granted and we got to do the full display and it felt fantastic to be performing in front of the home crowd so to speak with family and friends in attendance".

RIAT Fairford and the Lockheed Martin Cannestra Trophy

The Royal International Air Tattoo (known almost universally as 'RIAT') is held annually at RAF Fairford in Gloucestershire and is arguably the largest military air show in the world. The Silver Swallows were invited to perform at RIAT on 19/20 July 1997 in front of a crowd estimated at over 300,000 people and with a large gathering of military personnel from many nations. Little known outside the world of professional military aerobatic display flying, the Lockheed Martin Cannestra Trophy is awarded at RIAT each year to the best flying demonstration by an overseas participant. The winners of this award over the years have been many and varied, including both 'solo' displays and aerobatic teams; very well-known winners in the latter category have included the Italian Air Force's Frecce Tricolori, the Armée de l'Air's Patrouille de France and the Turkish Stars, representing that country's air arm. However, 1997 was to be the year of the Irish and the Silver Swallows pulled off an extraordinary achievement by winning the trophy that year. Paul Whelan recalls the events of that day;

"The display was performed on a baking hot day at Fairford and the thermals and turbulence were something else, with heat rising off the buildings and large expanses of concrete at the base. Graeme was hyper-enthusiastic about the display that day and his enthusiasm was caught on video because we had cameras on board. So enthusiastic was he that just after takeoff he pulled up

The success of the Silver Swallows was made possible through excellent teamwork by all in Light Strike Squadron.
Back Row L – R:
Captain P. McDonnell,
Sergeant M. Bambrick,
Lieutenant P. Whelan,
Captain G. Martin,
Lieutenant C. Keegan,
Corporal D. Ryan.
Front Row: L – R:
Airman M. Delaney,
Airman J. Delaney,
Airman G. Hilliard.
[Graeme Martin Collection]

Above: The 1997 Silver Swallows Display Team pose proudly with the Lockheed Martin Cannestra Trophy. [Graeme Martin Collection]

so quick that we lost him and ducked below and we had to work hard to get back to him. All our nerves settled after that and we relaxed into routine. All the practise during the previous months paid off and we flew a great display. I think it was mentioned in the notes afterwards that we really managed the turbulence quite well. At the end we were just so happy that we had done the display as well as we could".

Commandant Kevin Byrne was the Air Corps commentator at most of the Silver Swallows displays during that period, whether performing at home or overseas. He was scheduled to be the commentator at Fairford that day but was held up in traffic, having arrived in the UK separately from the rest of the team. He arrived just in the nick of time, barely making it in the gate as the Silver Swallows were lining up on the runway and had to bound up the stairs to the control tower just as they took off. Commandant Byrne was introduced to the spectators by the regular RIAT commentator Sean Maffett as the Silver Swallows' "silver–tongued devil" of a display commentator and – despite his somewhat unorthodox arrival – he managed to provide a faultless running commentary without any notes whatever to hand.

The announcement of the award did not come until the next evening as RIAT is a two day show, the team

flying on both days. As Paul Whelan remembers:

"Later on, we were at the post-display hangar party, hanging around with the Dutch after the dinner and in no way did we expect that we would win. Perhaps Graeme had an inkling but for the rest of us it was an absolute surprise when the award was announced. Naturally there was much celebration that evening and Kevin Byrne spent most of the night on the phone to the media back home telling them of our success. News of the award did get a few column inches in the evening papers and regional papers back home but didn't achieve as widespread coverage as we might have hoped. Nonetheless there were great celebrations back at Baldonnel when we brought the trophy home the following day".

Graeme Martin recalls the moments leading up to the announcement that the Silver Swallows had won the trophy;

"I remember having a beer with the other pilots, from different teams, outside an enormous tent that was set up for the air crew on the military apron so we could have an after show party. They announced that they wanted everyone inside, so that they could award the various prizes. I remember someone saying that there was no point in us going inside, as we would hardly win! And I remember saying to Pete to get the other members of the Team to go inside. I really wanted to see who would win. Who was better than us on the day? I knew that we were not the most spectacular team there (no smoke, etc), but I knew we had flown two flawless displays over the

Right: Heading for home. The Silver Swallows fly in a loose formation low over the Irish Sea when returning from a UK airshow.
[Sgt. Pat Cornally Photo]

two days. I knew our timings, positioning, formation, had been exact. I was especially aware that the judging panel were sitting right in the middle of the display line, and that all during our display we had nailed that position. I felt that we were at least as good as any other team there (from a professional and technical point of view), and better than others. However I do still remember the overwhelming delight when they announced us as the winners. When they said 'Silver Swallows', I had to look around to make sure I wasn't imagining it. The boys were speechless! I had a feeling we had a chance, but had said nothing to the lads. An incredible and proud day to be a member of the Irish Defence Forces".

The Silver Swallows continued displaying at home and abroad for the remainder of the 1997 season with a display at Florennes in Belgium on 7 September followed by a visit to RAF Leuchars in Scotland on 12 September. The final public display in Ireland took place at Shannon on 21 September and the very last display ever performed by the Silver Swallows was held later that evening directly over the Officers' Mess in Baldonnel in front of an audience of invited guests, families and friends. It was the end of a remarkable era of formation displays by the Air Corps.

Looking Back – The Achievements of the Silver Swallows

In all air arms throughout the world, display teams have three primary purposes: to enhance the public image of their respective air arms, to serve as a recruitment and public relations vehicle and to display the professionalism and dedication of all the pilots and ground staff who have trained in that organisation. There is no doubt that the Silver Swallows excelled in these areas, but they also brought pride to the Air Corps and to the personnel of Light Strike Squadron in particular, whose achievements were often overshadowed by their higher profile counterparts operating helicopters in No. 3 Support Wing. They also demonstrated what could be achieved by a very small, dedicated team with minimal resources. They could be considered to be one of Europe's finest aerobatic display teams as exemplified by the award of the Lockheed Martin Cannestra Trophy in their final season of operations. At a diplomatic level, there is no doubt that they enhanced the standing of Ireland, the personnel of the Silver Swallows being very aware of their ambassadorial roles and how their dedication and professionalism in flying and maintaining very old aircraft to an incredibly high standard would be perceived by their professional counterparts abroad.

The final word on this must go to John Mulvanny;
"I have had a very lucky career but looking back without a doubt I would say the best thing I have ever done in my career was the Silver Swallows. When you are young and you are interested in handling aircraft, which is what I was only ever interested in doing, the Silver Swallows was the ultimate in what you could do".

The award winning 1997 sequence as described by team leader Captain Graeme Martin

1. Arrive 30 degrees from display line (DL), from behind crowd line. Fly for approx. 30 seconds, depending on headwind or tailwind.

2. Pull up into a starboard wingover. This was varied in order to roll out onto the display line, (if we were too close I could always pull more g to roll out, or less g if were too far from the axis).

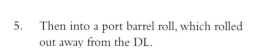

1+2

3. Two loops along the display line, one after the other.

4. Then we went into another starboard wingover to set up approx. 30 degrees to the DL in opposite direction.

3+4

5. Then into a port barrel roll, which rolled out away from the DL.

6. Then another starboard wing over to position along the DL.

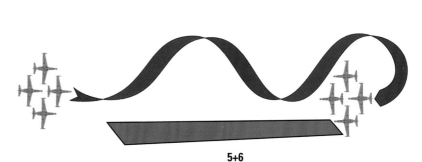

5+6

7. The Nos. 2 and 3 performed the 'Roll Back', and positioned in to 'Arrow formation'.

8. Then a wide low level turn so that we came back towards the DL, but at 90 degrees to it.

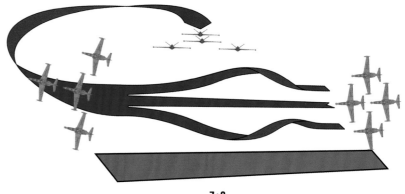

7+8

9. Then a loop in arrow formation straight toward the crowd line, however we had to perform a 120 degree starboard turn at the top in order not to roll out over the crowd.

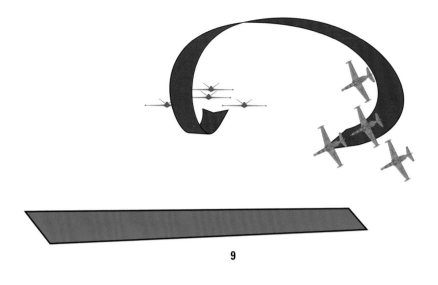

9

10. Then a tight low level port turn while returning to 'Diamond' formation. This then had us rolling out straight towards the DL, at 90 degrees to it.

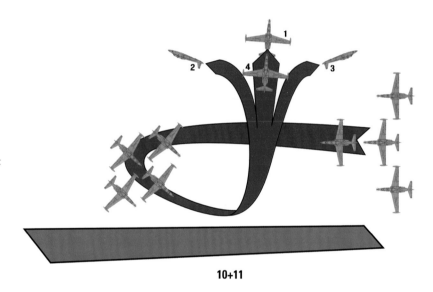

10+11

11. We would then pull up vertically, with the No. 4 staying line astern with me, as the No. 2 and 3 broke formation. We would then perform a roll off the top, that would take us away from the DL, while 2 and 3 flew at low level in opposite directions along the DL. Nos. 2 and 3 then performed port and starboard wing overs in order to return to the DL for the opposition pass. No. 2 (Pete McDonnell) would pick his flight line along the axis, while No. 3 (Paul Whelan) would scan the horizon for him, and call "in sight" when he had made visual contact. Pete would then maintain his line, while Paul would miss him! Very important that only one pilot is maneuvering!! At the moment they 'crossed' they would both snap into a tight turn and turn away from DL.

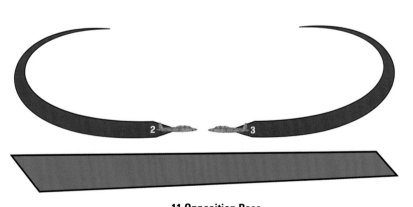

11 Opposition Pass

12. During this time myself and No. 4 (Chris Keegan) would be positioning for a Mirror Pass. We timed it to that we were just at the start of our run in as 2 and 3 were in their low level turn. Pete would call "clear" so I knew they were already turning.

13. As we (1&4) flew up the DL, I would pull up slightly and roll to port, to go inverted. Once inverted I would push neg g in order to maintain level flight, (for 30 seconds) while Chris accelerated from line astern to go as close as he could judge, with the aim of putting the nose of his aircraft between the 'V' tail of my aircraft. After 30 seconds, I would push as much negative g as I could take, and roll out, as No. 4 stayed in line astern.

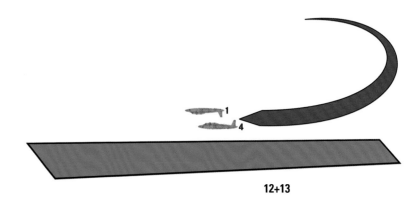

12+13

14. As we climbed away 2 and 3 would be on our tails in order to rejoin as a 'Diamond' formation. We were very proud of this as it was the only time the Swallows broke formation, and rejoined again to complete other manoeuvres.

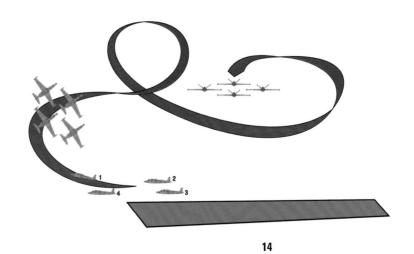

14

15. Then a loop along the DL to position for the final vertical manoeuvre which was a loop at 45 degrees to the DL and as we started the descent from the top of the loop we would perform a 'Bomb Burst' and each aircraft would break 90 degrees to each other. Another first for the Swallows.

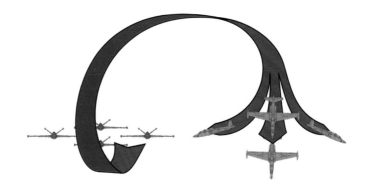

15

Irish Air Corps Fouga Magister Notable Displays

Year	Notable Air Displays	Leader	No.2	No.3	No.4
1979	Popes visit (Phoenix Park) Flypast only, 29 September 1979.	Comdt. P.Curley	Capt. B. Murphy	Lt. N. McHugh	2nd. Lt. A. Regan
1981	Air Spectacular (Fairyhouse) 16 August 1981 (Flypast only).	Comdt. Geoff White	Capt. Con Murphy	Lt. Dermot McCarthy	Lt. A. Regan
1982	Air Spectacular (Fairyhouse) 22 August 1982.	Capt John Flanagan	Lt. A. Regan	Lt. Dermot McCarthy	N/A
1983	Three-ship at Fairyhouse on 21 August 1983. 215, 216 and 220 (unofficial loop).	Comdt. John Flanagan	Lt. Tony Regan	Lt. Dermot McCarthy	N/A
1984	Solo display by Dermot McCarthy.	Lt. Dermot McCarthy			
1985	Three-ship planned for Air Spectacular in Cork 18 July 1985 (Cancelled).	Capt. Kevin Barry	Lt. John Kelly	Lt.John Mulvanny	
1986	Three-ship Formation Aerobatic display – Air Spectacular (Baldonnel) 17 August 1986.	Capt. Kevin Barry	Lt. John Kelly	Lt.John Mulvanny	
1987	Four-ship, Air Spectacular (Baldonnel), first appearance of Red Arrows in Ireland and first use of Silver Swallows name.	Capt. Kevin Barry	Capt. Jack Killoch	Lt. Pearse McCrann	Capt. A. Regan
1988	Four-ship, Abbeyshrule 7 August 1988, Air Spectacular (Baldonnel) 14 August 1988.	Capt. Kevin Barry	Capt. Jack Killoch	Lt.John Mulvanny	Lt. Pearse McCrann
1989	Four-ship Vinegar Hill 2 July 1989, Cork 5 July 1989, Foynes 8 July 1989, Abbeyshrule 6 August 1989, Newtownards 12 August 1989, Air Spectacular (Baldonnel) 13 August 1989.	Capt. Kevin Barry	Lt. John Kelly	Lt.John Hurley	Lt. John Mulvanny
1990	Four-ship Cork 10 July 1990, Air Spectacular (Shannon) 22 July 1990, Ringaskiddy (QE2) 23 July 1990, first overseas display at RAF Brawdy 26 July 1990.	Lt.John Mulvanny	Lt. Martin Duffy	Lt. Kieran Friel	Lt. John Kelly
1991	Only 220 available for solo aerobatics in 1991.	Capt. Martin Duffy			
1992	Various local displays.	Capt. John Kelly	Lt. Graeme Martin	Lt. Paddy McNamee	
1993	Salthill Airshow 27 June 1993 (Four-ship planned, but No. 4 unserviceable on start-up).	Capt. John Kelly	Lt. Rory O'Connor	Lt. Niall Connors	Capt Martin Duffy
1994	Formation display Clifden 15 June 1994 (75th Anniversary Alcock & Brown), Salthill Airshow 3 July 1994.	Capt. John Kelly	Capt Martin Duffy	Lt. Niall Connors	
1995	Abbeyshrule Airshow 13 August 1995.	Capt. John Kelly	Capt Martin Duffy	Lt. Niall Connors	
1996	Three-ship flypast followed by Solo display by Graeme Martin over USS John F. Kennedy.	Capt. Graeme Martin	Capt. Peter McDonnell	Lt. Paul Whelan	Lt. Christian Keegan
1997	Air Displays at RIAT Fairford – England, Leuchars – Scotland, Florennes – Belgium, Families Day at Baldonnel.	Capt. Graeme Martin	Capt. Peter McDonnell	Lt. Paul Whelan	Lt. Christian Keegan

Maintaining the Fouga

Light Strike Squadron was a small unit within the Air Corps. Apart from three to four pilots assigned to the squadron at any given time the establishment was usually one flight sergeant, one sergeant, four corporals, seven airmen and two to four apprentices but the number assigned could vary from this substantially. This small team worked wonders in making available at least four and occasionally five aircraft out of a fleet of six for the 'Wings' courses and displays by the Silver Swallows. It was a master feat of scheduling the

requisite maintenance checks that enabled Light Strike Squadron to have the required number of aircraft available. The Air Corps had a long history of training their own aircraft technicians at the Apprentice School which is now part of the Air Corps College. It was a much sought after career in the 1980s with as many as seven thousand applicants for as little as twenty places available each year. This cadre of highly skilled technicians were key to the operational maintenance of all of the aircraft flown by the Air Corps.

Five of the six Air Corps Fouga Magisters seeen here in the Light Strike Squadron Hangar at Baldonnel.
[Sgt. Pat Cornally Photo]

Above: Fouga Magister 219 undergoing a 150-hour check. Note the aircraft jacking points.
[Patrick J. Cummins Photo]

Paul Gibbons joined the Air Corps as a member of the 49th Apprentice class in 1985. After completing his training as an apprentice he was assigned to Light Strike Squadron. As Paul recalls, maintaining the Fouga was an interesting assignment:

"Maintaining the Fouga was a reasonably straightforward affair provided sufficient spare parts were available. Relatively little special equipment was required for servicing. Each technician would have three vital tools with which to service the Fouga, namely a twelve inch Philips head screwdriver, a canopy key and a hydraulic key. Ground equipment consisted of a Fouga-specific towbar, three ground power units and a small electric tow truck.

At the start of each day a daily inspection or D.I. was carried out on the aircraft scheduled to fly. This required the technicians to check all systems were functioning properly. For example, a small amount of fuel would be drained from each tank to ensure that it was not contaminated with water. Tyre pressures would be checked and flight controls would be checked for free movement. Every system was checked apart from actually doing a ground run of the engines. The daily inspection usually took about half an hour to complete. The pilot would also carry out his own pre-flight inspection, checking the aircraft externally and removing intake blanks and safety pins indicated by red 'remove before flight' tags. All items removed were laid out on a set pattern on the ground in front of the aircraft to ensure that all blanks and safety pins were accounted for.

All aircraft have a strict maintenance schedule based on the number of flight hours accumulated. For the Fouga, the first check occurred at 25 hours when the Cardan

shaft that links the main generator to the port engine required a heavy greasing. The next check was at 50 hours and this was mainly concerned with lubricating all moving parts with oil (flight control hinges) and grease (undercarriage). It would take about three hours to complete a 50-hour check. The 50-hour check was carried out again when the aircraft had accumulated 100 hours of flying time but a much more in-depth inspection was carried out at 150 hours. For the 150-hour inspection the aircraft was put up on jacks and a detailed inspection was carried out on every major component over a period of about two weeks. The cycle would repeat again up until the 300 hour flight time had been reached. The 300-hour inspection was even more detailed and required the engines to be removed. A thorough inspection of every system would be carried out, replacing time-expired or worn components. Aircraft could be on an extended 300-hour inspection for several months. If spare parts were in short supply then it was common for the aircraft that was on its 300-hour check to have parts removed and placed on the other aircraft to keep them serviceable. The cycle would repeat again until 600 hours of flying time had been accumulated. At 600 hours the aircraft underwent a complete disassembly (including wings removed) with a full structural inspection to ensure there were no fatigue cracks or corrosion in the airframe. X-ray equipment was used to examine the main spars in the wings. Items such as canopy seals were also replaced. Later on, as the aircraft reached the end of their service, non-destructive testing of the wing root joints were carried out on a scheduled basis. The 600-hour checks were mainly carried out by SOGERMA with the aircraft being fitted with the larger 230-litre tip tanks for the ferry flight to France.

Due to the exigencies of the service it was not always

possible to carry out the scheduled checks at exactly the 50 hour or 300 hour milestones. In such instances an extension would be applied for and permission was usually granted to postpone the maintenance check for a few hours. A typical example would be when an aircraft had to position away from Baldonnel for some reason and if a maintenance check came due then it would be postponed until the aircraft was back at Baldonnel.

If the engines were not to be used for an extended period of time they were "inhibited" prior to being stored in a nitrogen-filled container. Standard practice was for the engine to be ground run until sufficiently warmed up. The engine would be powered down and while still warm a mix of oil and fuel would be injected into the fuel lines while the engine was turning over, though not lit. This coated all interior surfaces with a light film of oil which inhibited corrosion. The nitrogen rich atmosphere in the container also helped to prevent corrosion. When it came time to refit the engines to the airframe the first engine run would be quite smoky as the oil film burned off the interior surfaces.

The Fouga was relatively easy to maintain. It helped if you had small hands as some of the access panels and hatches were quite small and you were sometimes working blind when carrying out adjustments or trying to apply oil or grease where needed. The way the Squadron operated you were assigned the role of crew member initially. This involved taking your daily taskings from the Flight Sergeant or NCO in charge. As your experience grew you got involved in more complex maintenance work. You would start off doing the 50-hour check or first line maintenance. Then you would progress on to second line maintenance (150-hour and 300-hour inspections) under the supervision of an NCO or more experienced Airman

who would be designated Crew Leader. Eventually you would be promoted to NCO and be given charge of up to three aircraft. The maintenance would be carried out by the Airmen, accounted for by the NCO in charge but ultimately signed off by the Flight Sergeant who was the aircraft inspector.

One of the perks of the job was getting to fly in the back seat of the Fouga. Usually this would be as a recorder for a test flight following the return to service of the aircraft after a 150-hour or 300-hour inspection. Occasionally the test flight would be required because some problem had cropped up outside of the normal maintenance cycle. These could get exciting and I remember on a couple of occasions being a recorder on test flights where the engines flamed out at high altitude, but still within what would be the normal operating height of the aircraft. The glide characteristics of the Fouga were excellent (1.18 glide ratio) and we glided down to 10,000 feet at which point both engines were successfully relit."

The Fouga in Detail

The Fouga Magister is an elegant aircraft and in this section we will describe in some detail much of the structure and systems of this remarkable trainer. For the most part the fuselage, wings and engines are described via the accompanying photos but there are some systems that are not externally visible but are worth describing here. The key dimensions and performance characteristics are provided in the accompanying table. All photos in this section by Radu Brînzan unless otherwise stated.

Above: 3-KE was the Fouga Magister instructional airframe. Although assigned the serial number 221, this was never applied to the airframe.
[Patrick J. Cummins Photo]

Fuel system

The fuel is located in two fuselage tanks, two wingtip tanks and one inverted-flight accumulator. The inverted-flight accumulator is operated by compressed air tapped from the engine, downstream of the compressor. This allows for 30 seconds of inverted flight at full throttle at sea level. The main fuel tanks are placed inside the fuselage and are interconnected. They are made of rubber though they are not self-sealing. The fuselage tanks are filled by an inlet on the upper fuselage behind the cockpit.

Capacity:	Front	255 litres (56 imp. gallons)
	Rear	475 litres (104 imp. gallons)
	Total	730 litres (160 imp. gallons)

The two streamlined wingtip tanks are made of metal and are non-jettisonable. Each tank is filled separately via a filler cap on the top side. The fuel from the wingtip tanks drains into the main fuel tank with the help of compressed air tapped from the engine, downstream of the compressor. Fuel can be jettisoned via an electrically-controlled dump valve at the rear of the tank. Capacity per tank 125 litres (27 Imp. gallons)

Oil system

Each engine is lubricated from two separate oil tanks located in the fuselage. Oil circulation is provided by pumps located on the engines, which draw oil from the two storage tanks. Each of these tanks has a capacity of 12.5 litres (22 pints).

Hydraulic system

The hydraulic system of the CM.170 is used for operating the undercarriage, the brakes, the landing flaps, the airbrakes, the machine gun charging and the aileron booster. During normal operation, the pressure of 241 bar (3500 psi) is provided by a pump installed on the accessory gear box driven by the left engine. The self-regulating pump regulates the pressure to that level regardless of the flow. The system uses two tanks installed downstream of the pump. The first tank (located near the pump) is used for storing liquid under pressure for all hydraulic ancillaries. The other tank (located in the front end of the aircraft) is used only for parking and emergency brakes.

During emergency operation, the pressure is provided by a hand pump in the front cockpit actuated by the pilot. The only functions that can be carried out with this pump are undercarriage extension and actuation of airbrakes.

The hydraulic liquid supplying both pumps is stored in a tank with the capacity of 6.5 litres (12 pints) of which 1.4 litres (2½ pints) are set aside for the emergency system.

Electrical system

The electrical installation of the CM.170 operates on 27.5 volt DC and is of the single-wire type with return by ground. Since most of the accessories have no built-in ground lead, the negative current is conducted by wire up to the nearest electrical box in which these negative wires are assembled and grounded. The power is supplied by a 2500 Watt generator installed on the accessory gear box, driven by the left engine. A 35 AH NiCad battery is charged permanently by the generator. A ground connector located above the right engine cowling is used for powering the installation from a ground power unit. An inverter supplying 3-phase 115 volt 400 Hz current is used for powering the gyro compass. Each of the radio units (VHF1 and VHF2) is supplied by an individual inverter.

Avionic Systems

The avionic systems fitted to the Fouga are relatively simple. Apart from two VHF radios, the Fouga is equipped with a VOR/DME navigational aid.

Right: The two large loop devices on the nose of the CM.170 are the antennas for the VOR. Note the covers over the gun openings.

Right: The radio hardware is stored under the clear dome at the rear of the cockpit. A metal sun shield is bolted underneath the Plexiglas to protect the radio units against the heat of the sun.

Above: The radio hardware units viewed from the back. The large unit on the left side of this image is a Rockwell Collins 51RV-1 VOR/ILS Receiver. The two units on the right side of this photo are Rockwell Collins VHF20A Receiver-Transmitter sets.

Top: The clear dome is hinged and can be easily opened for easy access to the radio hardware.

Below: Clear photo of the parachute worn by Fouga pilots.
[Comdt. Dave Corcoran Photo]

Safety systems

The CM.170 is equipped with a fire-detection installation in the jet engine compartments, but no extinguisher system. Both pilots have seat parachutes. See photograph on right. The hinged canopy of each cockpit may be jettisoned in flight in order to facilitate bailing out. The jettison controls are the same as for normal opening in the ground. Once the controls have been actuated, if the canopy does not pop up by itself, it only requires a push of less than 20 kg (40 lbs) to open. In case of crash-landing or an indisposition on the part of the pilot on the ground, the canopy can be opened using the emergency release. The emergency handles are located behind a thin Plexiglas panel between the two cockpits. To open the canopy, after breaking the glass the handles are pulled, which then open the canopies.

Below: Close-up of the emergency pull-handles used to jettison the canopies in the event of an emergency on the ground.
[Joe Maxwell Photo]

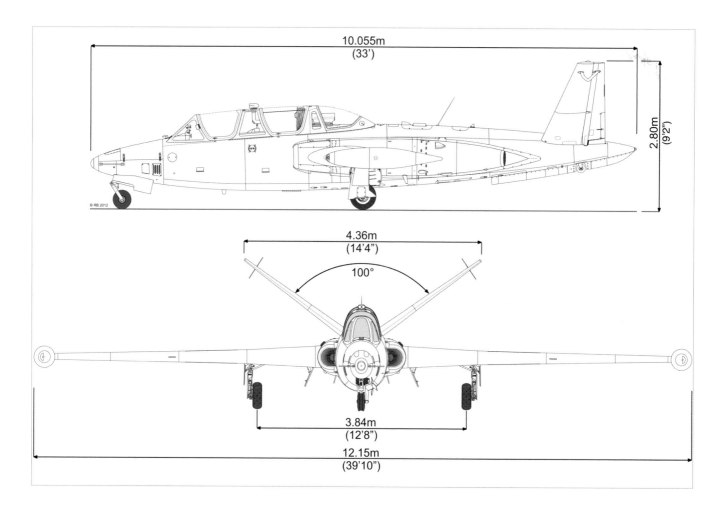

CM.170 Fouga Magister	
General characteristics	
Span, with tip tanks	12.15m (39' 10")
Span, without tip tanks	11.33m (37' 2")
Length	10.55m (33')
Maximum height on the ground	2.80m (9' 2")
Wing area	17.30m² (186,18 sq ft)
Wing loading, w/o armament, with full tip tanks	180 kg/m² (37 lbs per sq ft)
Airfoils: NACA laminar 64.200 series	
Tail unit: total area of the horizontal projection	3.75m² (92,2 sq ft)
Tail unit: opening angle 100°	
Empty weight, equipped	2140 kg (4720 lbs)
Total weight, w/o armament, w/o tip tanks	2900 kg (6400 lbs)
Total weight, w/o armament, with full tip tanks	3120 kg (6880 lbs)
Total weight, with guns, with full tip tanks	3160 kg (6960 lbs)
Performance	
Max. speed: 715 km/h (386 knots, 444 mph, 0.82 mach) at 9,000m (30,000 ft)	
Range: 925 km (500 nmi, 575 mi)	
Service ceiling: 11,000 m (36,080 ft)	
Rate of climb: 17 m/s (3,345 ft/min)	

Fuselage Details

Airflow diagram illustrating the various inlets and air vents.
The engine cowls feature a number of slots around the circumference that supply cooling air to the turbine box. The two smaller scoops at the top are inlets supplying cooling air to the compressed air line. The large scoop is the intake for the cooling air manifold. The access panel above it marked with a down-pointing black arrow is the cover for the ground power socket. The black tape prevents the engine covers from chafing the fuselage.
[With thanks to Paul Gibbons]

Scoops and vents:
1. Combustion chamber and jetpipe cooling intake
2. Rear bearing cooling intake
3. Front bearing cooling intake
4. Front rear bearing cooling vents
5. Oil tank cooling ramp (on fuselage centreline)
6. Combustion chamber and jetpipe cooling vent (passing between jetpipe and cowling)
7. Electrical generator cooling intake
8. Battery air scoops (x2)
9. Battery air vents (x2)

Covers:
A. Luggage compartment
B. Battery cover
C. Accessory gearbox / Battery compartment
D. Electrical generator
E. Hydraulic compartment
F. Port hydraulic accumulator
G. Starboard hydraulic reservoir
H. Main refuelling cap
I. Fuel igniter cover
J. Ground power unit connector on starboard side, oil fill on the port side.
[Paul Gibbons Photo]

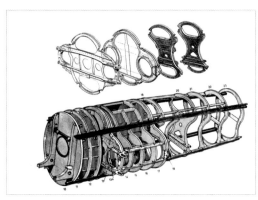

Fuselage structure diagram courtesy of EADS.

Fuselage Details

View of the fuselage with access panels removed. From left to right in this photo, the small panel behind the canopy is the main fuel tank filler, next to it is the access panel to the hydraulic reservoir, followed by a large access panel to the hydraulic pump and generator, then followed by the access panel to the equipment bay. Below these last two access panels, above the engine, is the access panel to the oil fill points. The engine can be easily serviced by removing the cowls. The attachment points for the engine cowls' dzus fasteners can be seen along the black anti-chafing tape.

On Right from top to bottom:

- Accessory gearbox and Battery compartment.
- Hydraulic compartment.
- Fuel Filler

Far Right:
The top of the fuselage features a number of large panels and scoops. The bullet-shaped intake leads to the hydraulic pump and the long semi-cylindrical scoops lead to the generator.

Below right: Luggage Compartment.

Far Right:
Two Pitot tubes are mounted ahead of the windscreen, one for each cockpit. The port head supplies the instruments of the front cockpit and the starboard head supplies the instruments in the rear cockpit. The curved panel at the bottom of the windscreen is the de-icing fluid sprayer.

Fuselage Details

Oil filler

Left Inset: View of the fuel control lines and main generator.

Right: The large fairing on the underside of the engine is the outlet for cooling air manifold. This also vents the bearing oil outlet, which explains the trail of grime behind it. The hole in the middle of the scoop is for the rear bearing oil drain. The large teardrop-shaped bulge covers the ignition plug and its wire. The fin-shaped outlet covers the injection pump vent and the baffle vent. The wedge-shaped ramp on the fuselage centreline is a cooling intake for the lubrication system. Behind, protruding under the fuselage, is the drain for the oil tanks.

Right: View of the fuselage underside looking forward. The fin antenna is a VHF antenna. The long slot at the joint between the engine pod and the fuselage is the lower boundary layer spill duct.

Left: Position lights are mounted in each wingtip fuel tank, green on the port side and green on the starboard side.

Left: A white (colourless) position light is mounted in the tail. The blue-coloured outlet is an air vent.

Left: A taxi light is mounted in the nose. Having a working light bulb was very important for formation aerobatics, particularly for the crossover manoeuvres.

Left: The oblong opening on the right side of the ventral fin is the outlet for the cockpit air conditioning system.

71

Wings and Empennage

View of the CM.170 wing towards the wing root showing the ailerons and flaps. The 'tufts' on the outboard end of the trailing edge of the ailerons are static discharge wicks. Aerodynamic compensation is also provided by an automatic tab. This tab is compensated by a mass balance counterweight. The trailing edge of the aileron, outboard of this tab, is blunted by a strip. The purpose of this strip is to increase resistance to flutter and reduce control forces at high speeds.

A stall strip can be seen on the leading edge of the wing, to the right of this photo. The purpose of this strip was to break the boundary layer airflow at high angles of attack and provide the pilot with some warning of the onset of a stall. The positioning of the stall strip created a vortex which flowed back over the aileron. The subsequent vibration provided the pilot with an indication of a possible stall condition.

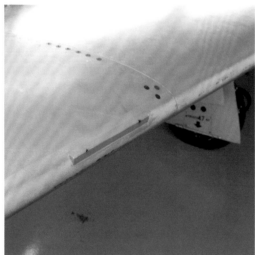

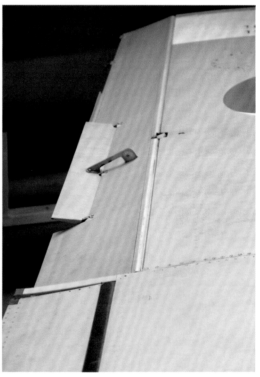

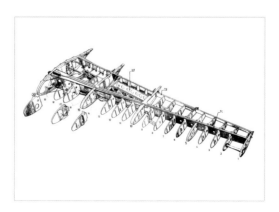

Internal structure of the CM.170 wing.
[Fouga CM.170 Magister Maintenance Manual, courtesy of EADS]

The automatic balance tabs are connected to the wing via a fixed rod and move in opposition to the aileron, i.e., when the aileron moves up, the tab moves down and when the aileron moves down, as shown here, the tab moves up. The mass balance of the tab moves through an opening in the wing. The mass balance serves to prevent aileron flutter.

Wings and Empennage

View of the sealing fabric, accessed via a hinged service panel on the underside of the wing. The purpose of this fabric is to prevent air flowing between the lower and the upper surfaces of the wing through the slots that exist between the wing surface and the aileron. This type of aerodynamic compensation was known as 'sealed aileron'. The actuation rod of the automatic tab is visible on the left edge of the photo.

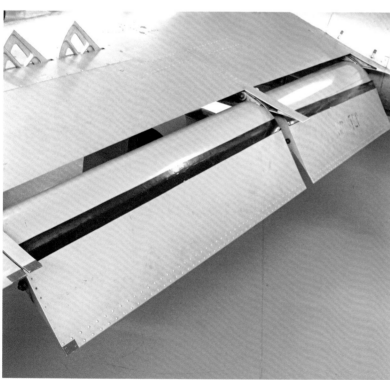

Flaps move on rollers located at the flap ends running on curved guide rails fitted to the ends of the wing ribs. The two flap sections in each wing are synchronised and move as a single unit. They are electrically controlled and hydraulically operated. The black strips visible in this photo are tapes that prevent chafing between the flaps and the wings.

The deployed flaps viewed from underneath. The maximum deflection of the flaps is 40° and the angle of deflection is indicated by a dedicated gauge in the cockpit. Note the hydraulic rams and the curved guide rails behind them.

Wings and Empennage

Below: The airbrakes are electrically controlled and hydraulically operated. These consist of two units of six perforated plates, one unit per wing, with all six plates of each unit mechanically synchronised to move in tandem. They do not have any pre-set settings or position gauge and can be extended or retracted as needed with the help of a rocker switch located on the throttle lever. Control priority is given to the rear cockpit (instructor) who can switch-off the current arriving at the switch in the front cockpit, overriding the pupil's action. This photo shows the airbrakes deployed, viewed from the back.

The photo below shows the partially-deployed airbrakes viewed from the front. Note that the pattern on the forward-facing side is different from the pattern on the rear side.

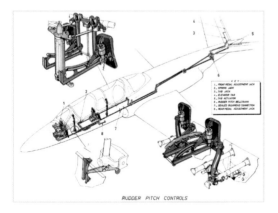

Above: Schematic diagram of the rudder/elevator controls. The rudder pedals control yaw and the forward/back movement of the control column control pitch.
[Image and text source: Fouga CM.170 Magister Maintenance Manual, courtesy of EADS]

Right: View of the port rudder/elevator. Note the trim tabs and mass balance counterweights. The trim tabs are electrically operated and controlled by a switch on each control column. A section of each rudder/elevator trailing edge is thickened by a strip to prevent flutter. The mass balance counterweight is secured to the rudder/elevator and moves through openings in the fixed tailplanes. The 'tufts' on the trailing edge of the rudder/elevator are static discharge wicks.

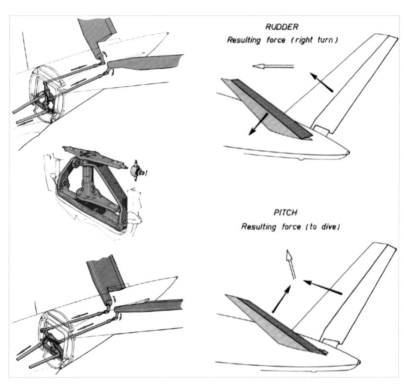

Above: Schematic diagram showing the operation of the rudders/elevators with the help of the tailplane differential unit. The purpose of this assembly is to translate the control motions made by the pilot in the elevator and rudder controls into simultaneous or differential movements of the moving parts of the butterfly-type tail unit. The trapeze-shaped frame highlighted in red is connected by rods to the control columns and can only pivot on the horizontal axis. The lever highlighted in green is connected by rods to the pedals and can pivot on the vertical axis, according to the movement of the pedals, on bearings secured to the frame highlighted in red, but can also tilt on the horizontal axis together with the trapeze-shaped frame.

Front Cockpit – list of items

1. Clock
2. Emergency compass
3. Parking brake
4. Machmeter
5. Gunsight
6. De-icer pump
7. Fire warning
8. Fuel gauge
9. Emergency compass light
10. Tachometer
11. Servo control switch
12. Air Speed Indicator
13. Artificial Horizon
14. Rate of Climb
15. Accelerometer
16. Landing gear warning
17. Fuel pressure warning
18. Tail pipe Indicators
19. Altimeter
20. Gyrocompass
21. Turn Indicator
22. Radio Compass
23. Emergency fuel warning
24. Machine Gun re-arming switch
25. Emergency bomb release
26. Landing Gear Control switch
27. Landing gear position indicator
28. Oil temperature
29. Landing flap position
30. Oil Pressure gauge
31. Cockpit altitude
32. Oxygen regulator
33. Pitot tube heater light
34. –
35. Pitot heater switch
36. Gyro horizon switch
37. Gyrocompass switch
38. Generator light
39. Generator switch
40. Battery switch
41. Battery circuit breaker
42. Gunsight rheostat
43. Armament selector panel
44. Rocket selector panel
45. U.V. light
46. Emergency panel lighting
47. Elevator tab indicator
48. U.V. light
49. Emergency panel lighting
50. Hydraulic pressure gauge
51. Voltmeter
52. Pedal adjustment
53. Emergency landing gear switch
54. Emergency airbrake selector
55. Throttle
56. Airbrake control switch
57. Throttle locks
58. Fuel cut-off cocks
59. Injection and ignition switch
60. Console lighting switch
61. Air conditioning indicator
62. Landing flap switch
63. Navigation light switch
64. U.V. light switch
65. Air conditioning switch
66. Landing light switch
67. Rheostat for emergency lighting
68. U.V. rheostat
69. Console lighting switch

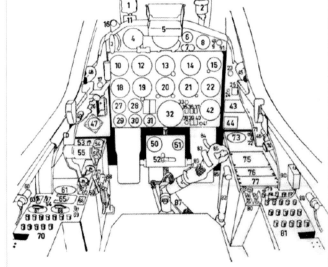

70. Electric circuit breakers
71. Intercom-lighting
72. Intercom-lighting rheostat
73. VHF 2 switch
74. Fresh air pickup
75. Radio compass control box
76. Intercom control box
77. VHF 1 control box
78. Starting light
79. Starter switch
80. Dump valve switch
81. Electric circuit breaker
82. Hand pump
83. Elevator tab control
84. Machine gun triggers
85. Bomb control switch
86. Gyro sight caging
87. Oxygen hose
88. Console light
89. Press-to-talk button
90. Radio junction box
91. Canopy control light

Above: Comparison between the factory-supplied front instrument panel and the subsequent modifications made to the Irish CM.170. The gunsight depicted in the factory drawing appears to be a Ferranti or Sperry gyroscopic gunsight, a device that was not used on the Irish CM.170. On the Irish CM.170, the radio compass and the turn indicator dials swapped locations. The gunsight rheostat was removed and replaced with the VOR display. Obscured by the control column in this photo, a set of three ILS marker lights, white for inner (airways) marker, blue for outer marker and amber for middle marker, were mounted above the cockpit altitude gauge. The gyrocompass and the artificial horizon dials were replaced with units of an improved design and were mounted on a separate panel standing proud of the main instrument panel. The altimeter was replaced with a unit of an improved design. On this aircraft [216], the accelerometer was replaced with a clock - it is unclear whether this was a modification implemented on all airframes.
[Image source: Fouga CM.170 Magister Maintenance Manual, courtesy of EADS].

Front Cockpit

Above: Forward view of the front cockpit showing the instrument panel, control column and rudder pedals. Note the standby compass mounted on the right side of the windscreen frame and the empty clock bracket on the left side of the windscreen frame. The piece of white paper to the left of the gunsight mount is a compass correction chart.

Above: A CM.170 control stick grip is on display in the Irish Air Corps Museum in Casement Aerodrome, Baldonnel.

Above: Three-quarter view of the left side front cockpit showing the throttle levers, fuel cut-off cocks, control column and part of the instrument panel. The red handle is the canopy release lever. Note the instrument panel lamp above it. A set of three ILS Marker lights, white, blue and amber, can be seen above the cockpit altitude gauge, behind the control column grip.

Above: View of the right side of the front cockpit showing the complete side console. Another bank of circuit breakers is housed at the rear end of the side console. The green hose is the oxygen supply. The small handle with a red button at the right of the seat is the seat height adjustment lever.

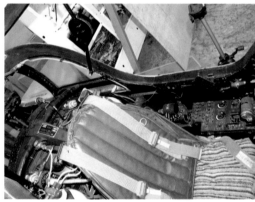

Above: Three-quarter rear view of left side of the front cockpit showing the rear of the left console with the circuit breaker panel and light controls. The yellow and black striped object secured to the left console is an emergency tool intended to break the canopy glass. Note the non-standard seat cushion taking the place usually occupied by a seat-parachute.

Front Cockpit

Top view of the entire cockpit canopy. The curved clear panels are made of Plexiglas and the flat windscreen is made of laminated tempered glass. Note the canopy hinges and the prominent binocular periscope.

Upper Left: Each pilot is secured to the seat by an adjustable five-point harness. The centre clasp can be turned in either direction to release the harness. Note the seat made of a laminated composite material, which is very similar to the type of material used on Spitfire seats.

Left: Three-quarter view of the right side front cockpit showing the right console housing the radio controls. The handle with a red knob is the emergency hydraulic hand pump.

Below: Rear view of the front cockpit. The two white bottles behind the seat are the breathing oxygen bottles. The seat cushion is not a standard item, that space was usually occupied by the parachute pack. The yellow and black striped object secured to the left console is an emergency tool intended to break the canopy glass.

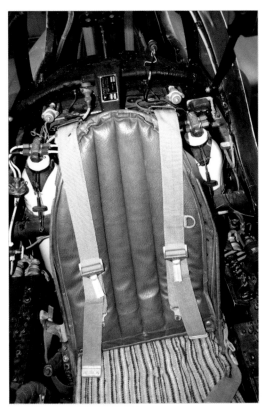

Rear Cockpit

Left: A view of the forward side of the rear cockpit showing the canopy frame, binocular periscope, instrument panel, rudder pedals and control column (the grip of the control column has been removed). The two white breathing oxygen bottles can be seen outboard of the rudder pedals. The 4DYK code is a remainder of the markings worn previously when this particular aircraft served in the Austrian Air Force. The Irish code 216 below it is the current identifier.

Above: To improve the instructor's visibility, the rear cockpit is provided with a binocular periscope. This periscope provides the instructor with a clear line of sight over the canopy. The periscope is fixed and can only provide a view forward.

Above: Open canopies viewed from the front. Note the handles and the rear-view mirrors.

View of the left side console with the throttles (partially covered by the cockpit lamp) and the fuel cut-off cocks. The yellow and black striped device is an emergency tool intended to break the canopy glass. The red handle is the canopy release. The large electrical box at the rear of the side console is the gyro-compass amplifier.

Rear Cockpit

Left: Top view of the rear cockpit showing the rear pressure bulkhead, seat and the canvas canopy hood. This canvas hood could slide forward on two tubular rails in order to simulate low visibility conditions during instrument flying instruction. Note the radio cables on the starboard side of the bulkhead. The blue line on the other side of the bulkhead supplies compressed air to the inflatable canopy seal, which can be seen on the left edge of this image.

Left middle: View of the right side of the cockpit showing the side console. The two dials are radio frequency selectors. The green tube is the oxygen supply.

Above: Top view of the clear dome covering the radio units. A thin metal-sheet sunshield is bolted inside the dome. The dome is hinged and can be swung up to allow for servicing the radios. The blue pipes are air vents, connecting the two main fuel tanks and the inverted flight fuel accumulator.

Left: The canopies are held up by spring-loaded articulated supports. The springs are housed inside large cylindrical boxes. The red cylinder on the left of the picture is the lock that secures the canopy support in the open position. The blue line running along the middle canopy frame supplies compressed air to inflatable seals around the edge of the canopy. The thin cable behind it is part of the mechanism that releases the deflection baffles on the windscreen when the canopies are jettisoned in an emergency. Note the canopy hinges and the rear of the binocular periscope.

Main Landing Gear

Above: The landing gear is protected by two outboard landing gear doors and one inner door. The main wheel doors have a chamois coloured paint on their inner surfaces. The wheel-wells are aluminium in colour. [John McFarland Photo]

Above: Front view of main landing gear leg. Note the way the two outboard undercarriage doors are offset from each other.

Above: The landing gear pivot point viewed from inboard - the front of the aircraft is to the left of the picture. The large polished metal bar to the left of the picture is the hydraulic retraction jack. Note the brake lines diverted around the retraction jack joint.

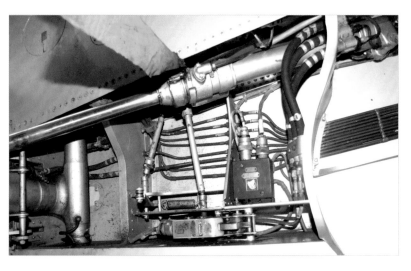

Above: View of the outboard section of the wheelwell roof - the front of the aircraft is at the top of this picture. The hydraulic lines supplying the retraction jack and the brakes occupy most of this space. The metallic rectangular box on the rear wall of the wheel well is the up-lock that secures the landing gear in the stowed position.

Landing gear and brakes

The retractable tricycle landing gear is manufactured by Messier. All three landing gear units are oleo-pneumatically damped and all three landing gear units are retracted hydraulically. Only the main wheels are fitted with hydraulically operated brakes. The brakes are controlled by the rudder pedals and can be used differentially for steering during taxiing. For emergencies or parking, the pilot in the front cockpit can use the parking brake handle on the top left of the instrument panel.

Main Landing Gear

The main landing gear viewed from the rear showing the hydraulic retraction jack and forward wheel well details. The pear-shaped plate secured to the centre of the hub engages the main landing gear retraction lever during the retraction sequence.

View of the inboard section of the wheelwell roof - the front of the aircraft is at the top of this picture. This section houses the wheel when retracted. The chamois-coloured item to the right of this picture extending into the wheelwell is the retraction lever for the inboard landing gear door. When pushed by the pear-shaped plate in the centre of the wheel hub, this item retracts the main landing gear door to close the well.

The inboard wall of the wheel well viewed from the rear - the front of the aircraft is to the left of this picture. The main wing spar forms the forward wall of the wheel well.

View of the inboard wall of the wheel well. The front of the aircraft is at the right of this picture. The inboard landing gear door retraction levers occupy most of this area. The chamois-coloured tube at the rear of the wheel well is the flap torque shaft.

Nose Wheel

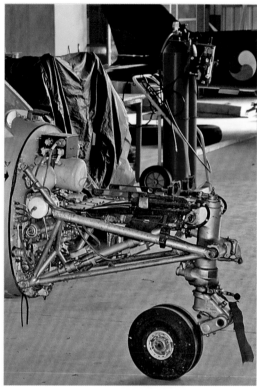

Above and Above Left:
Two views of the nose
wheel assembly.
[Patrick J. Cummins Photos]

Right: The nosewheel and
the levered suspension
axle seen from the left. The
metal rod extending from
the suspension lever to
the ground is an anti-static
line that earths the aircraft.
The red toggle is the
nosewheel steering lock.
When disengaged by hand
(as in this image), it allowed
the nosewheel to swivel
like a castor wheel, which
was a useful feature during
ground handling.

Above Right: A part of the
nose landing gear door is
split and folds upward in
order to provide clearance
for the nose landing gear
suspension lever that may
swing up to that extent
during harder landings.
The gills are vents for the
evacuation of gas and heat
from the spent ammunition
collection box. The door to
the left of the gills provides
access to the spent
ammunition box.

Above: The nosewheel and the levered
suspension axle seen from the right. The
tyre is solid rubber.

Inside view of the nose landing gear door showing the
retraction mechanism for the door itself as well as the split
door flap.

Nose Wheel

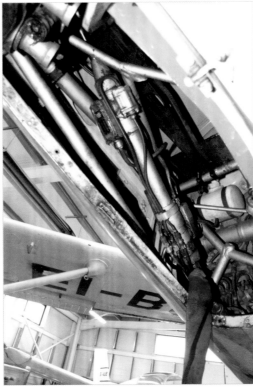

Left: View up inside the starboard side of the nose landing gear bay, looking towards the rear of the aircraft. The large silver-coloured object in the middle of the picture is the hydraulic retraction jack - a red 'Remove Before Flight' warning streamer is attached to the joint of the jack to the internal frame. The black item at the top of the wheel well is the machine gun mount.

Far Left: View up inside the nose wheel well looking forward. The two short cylinders at the back of the nose landing gear are anti-shimmy dampers. The silver-coloured 'Y' shaped object is part of the internal structure, while the multi-part silver-coloured object to the left of it is the linkage mechanism connecting the door retraction mechanism to the nose landing gear. The hydraulic jack is visible to the right of the wheel well. The jack is connected to the top of the nose landing gear, above the pivot point, which is located slightly above the anti-shimmy dampers.

The 'tail-wheel' inside the cut-out in the ventral fin is a device against over-rotation intended to prevent damage to the tail during a take-off rotation exceeding 5°.

There are hinged doors ahead of the wheel. These doors provided access to the rear fuselage jacking point. A pair of similar hinged doors is also present behind the wheel. Together with the front doors, they offer better service access to the wheel. Technicians would regularly place a piece of masking tape on the tail wheel concealed within the wheel bracket. If the tape was missing following a flight it could indicate that the aircraft had been over rotated, resulting in the tail wheel striking the runway!

Engine

The Marboré VI engine can be serviced easily by removing the entire engine cowling. The exhaust pipe is covered by a heat shroud, which is dimpled in order to increase the cooling area. The black tape is used to prevent chafing at the meeting point between the engine cowling and the fuselage. The engines are angled - each engine tailpipe is pointing out at 5° from each other on the horizontal plane and 2° down from the aircraft axis in the vertical plane.

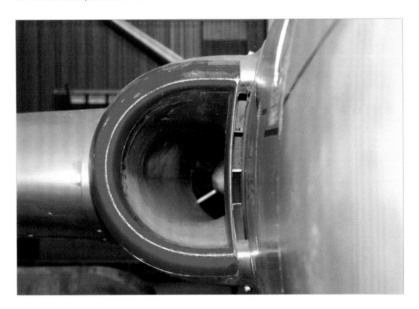

View down the engine intake showing the compressor vanes. A boundary layer splitter plate can be seen between the intake and the fuselage. Note the baffles that split the air into four separate channels, two leading to the top and two leading to the bottom.

View of the boundary layer spill duct on the top of the engine pod. An identical spill duct was also fitted on the underside. The purpose of the boundary layer splitter was to prevent turbulence close to the fuselage wall, which could affect the smooth flow of air to the engine. Note the divider in the middle.

Engine

Above:
Three views of a Marboré VI F2 engine. This is on display at the Irish Air Corps Museum.

Left
View of the underside of the engine.

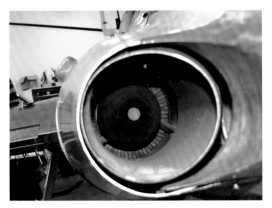

Far Left:
View of the exhaust nozzle showing the turbine vanes.

Left and Centre:
Views of the internal structure of the engine cowlings.

Wing Tip Fuel Tanks

For longer flights, the CM.170 could be fitted with larger ferry tanks with a capacity of 230 litres (50 imp. gallons). Unlike the normal tanks that were made of metal, these tanks are made of a composite material. In 1996 the French Air Force prohibited the use of the 230 litre tip tanks for installation on the Fouga because they found some cracks in the composite material at the root of the front tank attachment. Prior to 1996, these tanks had to be stripped of the paint every 18 months and inspected for cracks, hence the tanks here are unpainted.
[Christopher Roche Photo]

Right: The wingtip tanks were not jettisonable, but they could be removed for servicing. The oval access panel at the top of the tank is the refill point. The small metal protrusion on the side of the tank is the rear lock that secured the tank to the wing. The tanks have a capacity of 125 litres (27 Imp. gallons).

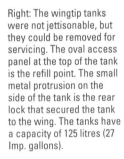

Above: The wingtip tanks are secured to the wing by a support spigot at the front and by a locking pin at the rear. The wingtip and wing joint is usually faired-over by a metal shroud. The bright red paint in this photo is the part that was protected by this shroud, while the outer unprotected area was bleached by the sun.

Above: On a couple of occasions, Fouga 219 was flown without wingtip tanks fitted. The flight characteristics were reported to be very different from that of the standard fitment.
[Sgt. Pat Cornally Photo]

Weapons

The gun barrels viewed from the side. The machine guns were used on the CM.170 during target practice, but usually the guns were removed and the gun openings were covered by special covers.

Above:
Fully armed Fouga, flown by Commandant John Flanagan. As seen here the Fouga could be armed with 68mm rockets in under wing pods and two 7.62mm machine guns in the nose.
[Air Corps Photo Section]

Centre left:
General layout of the AA-52 machine guns and ammunition feed. The rounds are stored in two boxes behind the guns from where they are carried in self-disintegrating link belts via curved feed chutes to the gun where they are fed from the left. After firing, the spent cases and links are ejected to the right through chutes and collected via hoppers in boxes on the sides of the nose wheel well.
[Image source: Fouga CM170 Magister Maintenance Manual, courtesy of EADS]

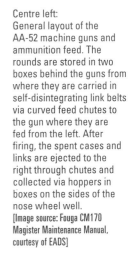

Left: Three-quarter rear view of the machine guns. To service the machine guns, the top nose panel can be removed by releasing four latches. The collection hopper for the spent cases and links from the right machine gun can be seen to the right. The collection devices are incomplete on both guns, the chutes leading from the ejection ports to the hoppers are missing. The shelf behind the guns is the support for the ammunition cases.

Chapter 6 — Maintaining the Fouga

Weapons

Right: The collection chute for the spent cases and links from the left-side machine gun can be seen between the two machine guns. The large device ahead and below the gun mounts is the top of the nose landing gear leg.

Machine guns

Two 7.62 mm AA-52 machine guns manufactured by MAS (Manufacture d'armes Saint-Étienne) in France can be installed in the front section of the fuselage. There is one ammunition box per machine gun, each holding 200 cartridges. The links and cartridges are recovered in two boxes placed under the guns. Firing is controlled by pressing the trigger on the control column. The machine guns can be re-armed with the help of a hydraulic charger controlled by a switch in the cockpit.

Action:	Delayed blowback
Rate of fire:	900 rounds per minute
Effective range:	600 metres (~2000 ft)
Maximum range:	3200 metres (~10,500 ft)
Total length:	1,166 mm (45.9 in)
Barrel Length:	600 mm (23.6 in)

Above: Side view of the machine guns. The chute leading from the hopper to the collection box for spent ammunition and links can be seen below the gun mounts. Note the cylindrical recoil damper.

Right: The gun mounts with the guns removed. The large cylindrical objects with long cut-outs are the hydraulic gun charging devices. The black box is an electrical junction box. The white container with two green stripes behind the ammunition box shelf is the windscreen de-icing fluid reservoir. The cylindrical box above it is the overpressure valve and the larger cylinder alongside it is the cockpit pressure regulator, both of which are part of the cockpit pressurisation system.

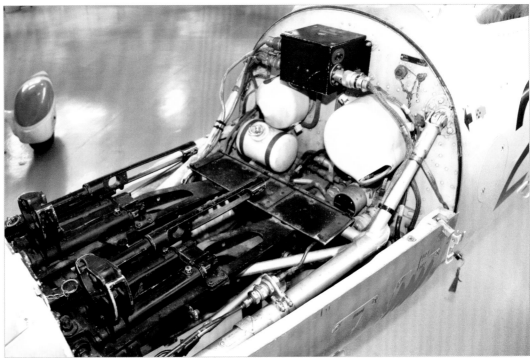

88

Above and Left: View of the MATRA F2 rocket pod. The pod consists of six hollow smooth-bore tubes holding the rockets, all placed in a radial layout inside an aerodynamically-shaped housing.
The red cap at the back covers the electrical socket for the firing cable. The two lugs at the top secure the pod to the specially-dedicated rack.

Left: View of the rocket pod on its pylon.
[Patrick J. Cummins Photo]

Far Left: The Irish Air Corps CM.170 used the Collimateur Type 83A3 gunsight manufactured by SFOM (Sociéte Francaise d'Optique et de Mècanique), the Optical Division of the French company Engins MATRA. This is a view of the gunsight viewed from the front.
[Sgt. Pat Cornally Photo]

Pilot's view of the gunsight. The sight line is fixed relative to the aircraft in azimuth. The vertical scale on the side is used to adjust the depression angle of the gunsight relative to speed and height. The circular dial on the front is used to adjust the sighting head.
[Sgt. Pat Cornally Photo]

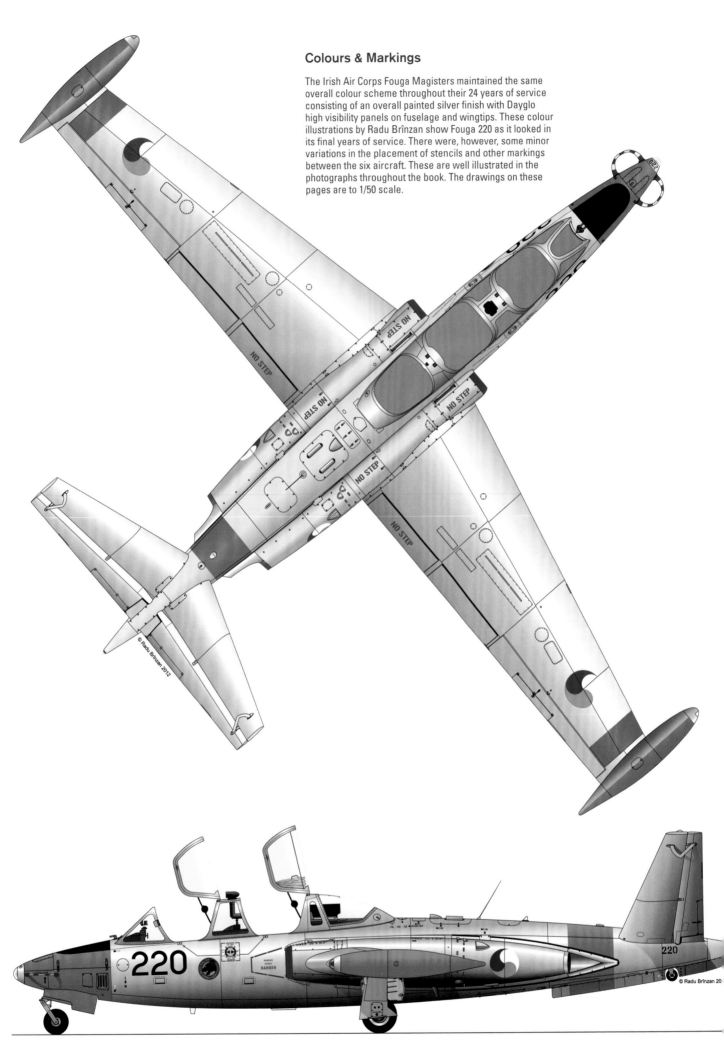

Colours & Markings

The Irish Air Corps Fouga Magisters maintained the same overall colour scheme throughout their 24 years of service consisting of an overall painted silver finish with Dayglo high visibility panels on fuselage and wingtips. These colour illustrations by Radu Brînzan show Fouga 220 as it looked in its final years of service. There were, however, some minor variations in the placement of stencils and other markings between the six aircraft. These are well illustrated in the photographs throughout the book. The drawings on these pages are to 1/50 scale.

© Radu Brînzan 2012

© Radu Brînzan 20

© Radu Brinzan 2012

© Radu Brinzan 2012

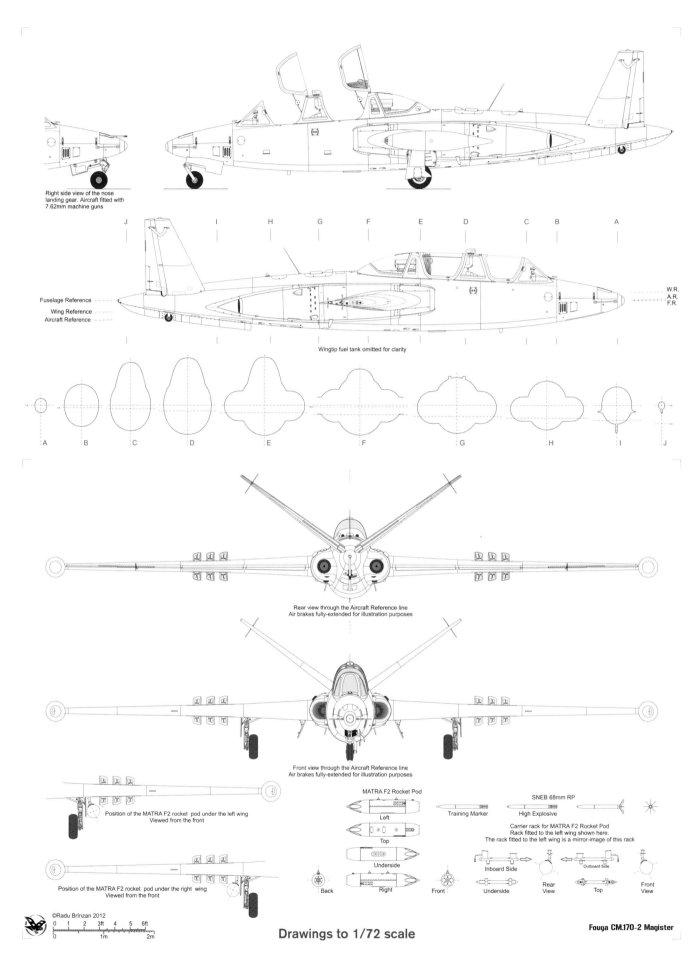

Right side view of the nose
landing gear. Aircraft fitted with
7.62mm machine guns

Fuselage Reference
Wing Reference
Aircraft Reference

W.R.
A.R.
F.R.

Wingtip fuel tank omitted for clarity

Rear view through the Aircraft Reference line
Air brakes fully-extended for illustration purposes

Front view through the Aircraft Reference line
Air brakes fully-extended for illustration purposes

Position of the MATRA F2 rocket pod under the left wing
Viewed from the front

Position of the MATRA F2 rocket pod under the right wing
Viewed from the front

MATRA F2 Rocket Pod

Left

Top

Underside

Back   Right   Front

SNEB 68mm RP

Training Marker   High Explosive

Carrier rack for MATRA F2 Rocket Pod
Rack fitted to the left wing shown here.
The rack fitted to the left wing is a mirror-image of this rack

Inboard Side   Outboard Side

Underside   Rear View   Top   Front View

©Radu Brînzan 2012

0 1 2 3ft 4 5 6ft
0   1m   2m

Drawings to 1/72 scale

Fouga CM.170-2 Magister

92

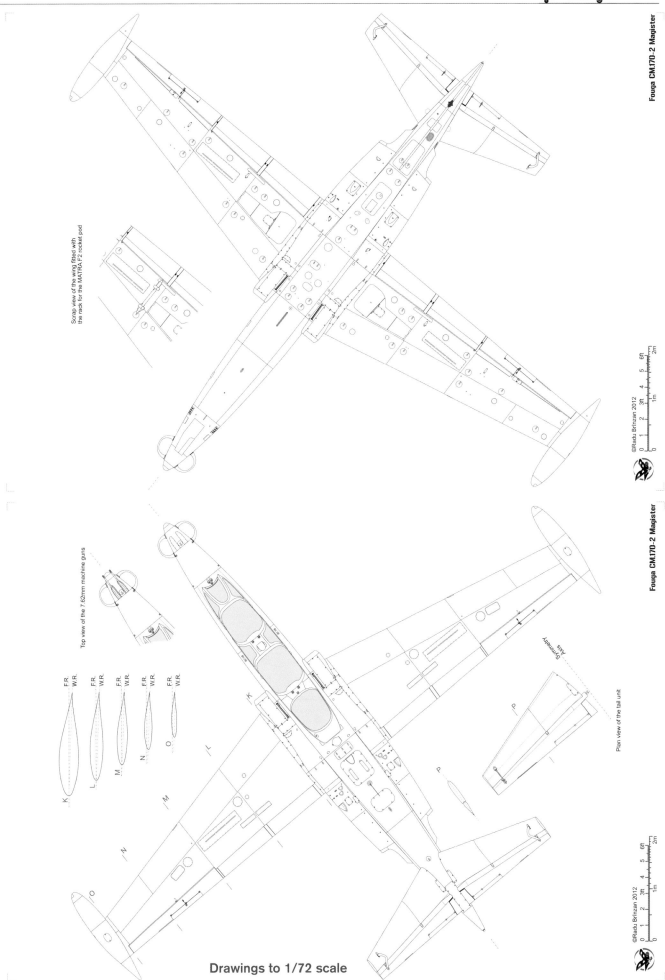

Scrap view of the wing fitted with
the rack for the MATRA F2 rocket pod

Top view of the 7.62mm machine guns

F.R.
W.R.

F.R.
W.R.

F.R.
W.R.

F.R.
W.R.

F.R.
W.R.

K

L

M

N

O

K

L

M

N

O

K

L

M

N

O

Symmetry
Axis

Plan view of the tail unit

P

P

Fouga CMJ70-2 Magister

©Radu Brînzan 2012

©Radu Brînzan 2012

Drawings to 1/72 scale

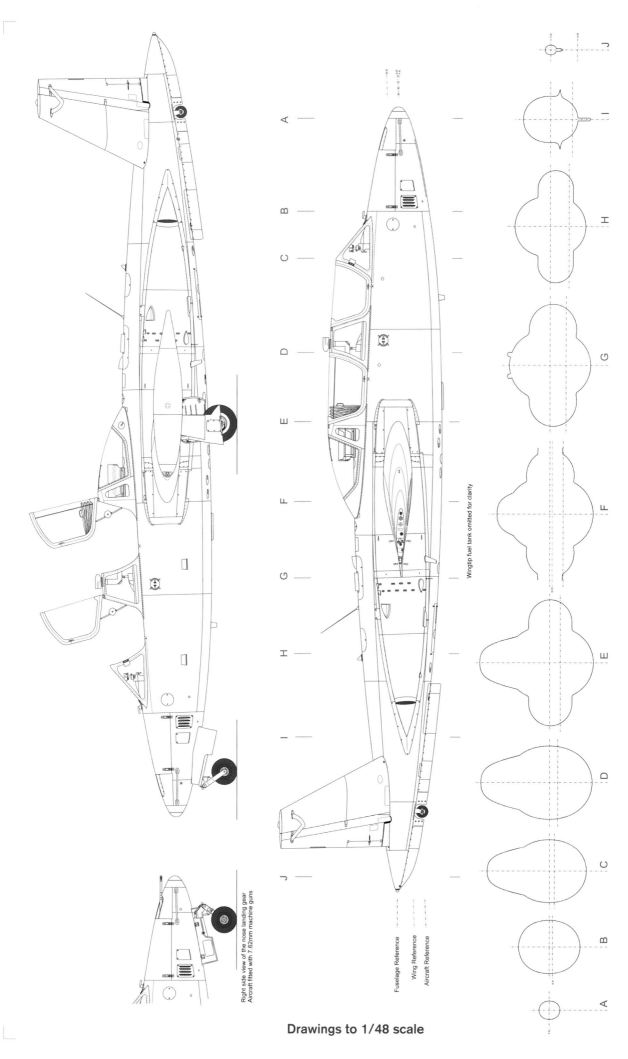

Right side view of the nose landing gear
Aircraft fitted with 7.62mm machine guns

Fuselage Reference
Wing Reference
Aircraft Reference

Wingtip fuel tank omitted for clarity

A   B   C   D   E   F   G   H   I   J

A   B   C   D   E   F   G   H   I   J

J   I   H   G   F   E   D   C   B   A

Drawings to 1/48 scale

Fouga CM.170-2 Magister

©Radu Brînzan 2012

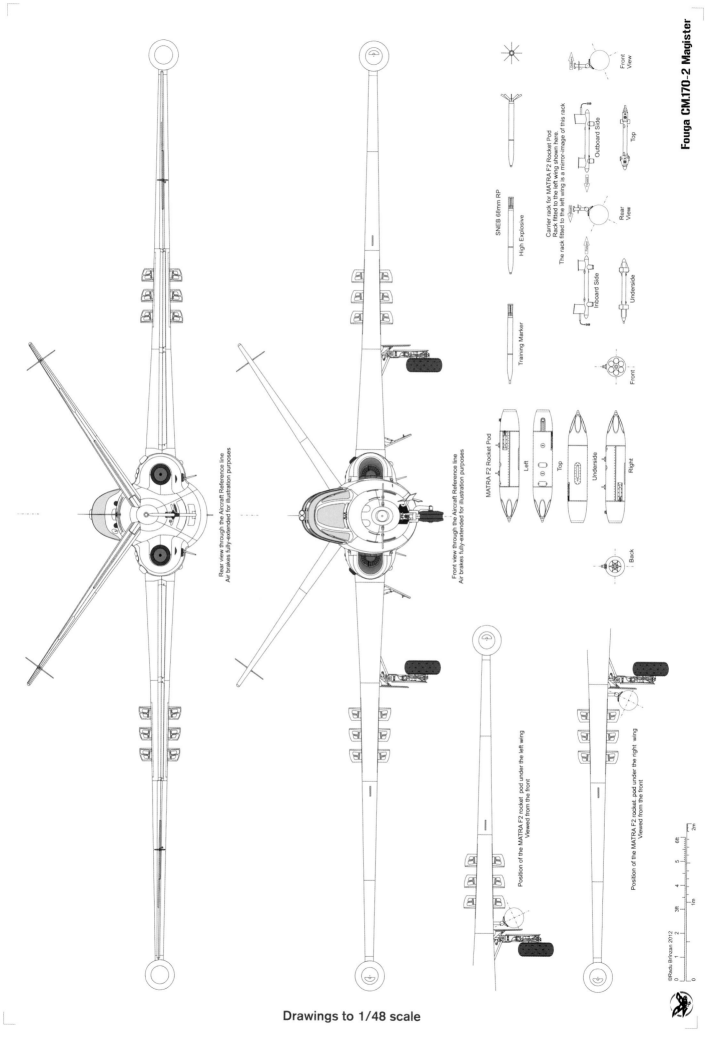

Rear view through the Aircraft Reference line
Air brakes fully-extended for illustration purposes

Front view through the Aircraft Reference line
Air brakes fully-extended for illustration purposes

SNEB 68mm RP

High Explosive

Training Marker

Carrier rack for MATRA F2 Rocket Pod
Rack fitted to the left wing shown here.
The rack fitted to the left wing is a mirror-image of this rack

Front View

Outboard Side

Top

Rear View

Inboard Side

Underside

Front

MATRA F2 Rocket Pod

Left

Top

Underside

Right

Back

Position of the MATRA F2 rocket pod under the left wing
Viewed from the front

Position of the MATRA F2 rocket pod under the right wing
Viewed from the front

©Radu Brinzan 2012

0   1   2   3ft   4   5   6ft   1m   2m

Drawings to 1/48 scale

Fouga CM.170-2 Magister

95

Drawings to 1/48 scale

Scrap view of the wing fitted with
the rack for the MATRA F2 rocket pod

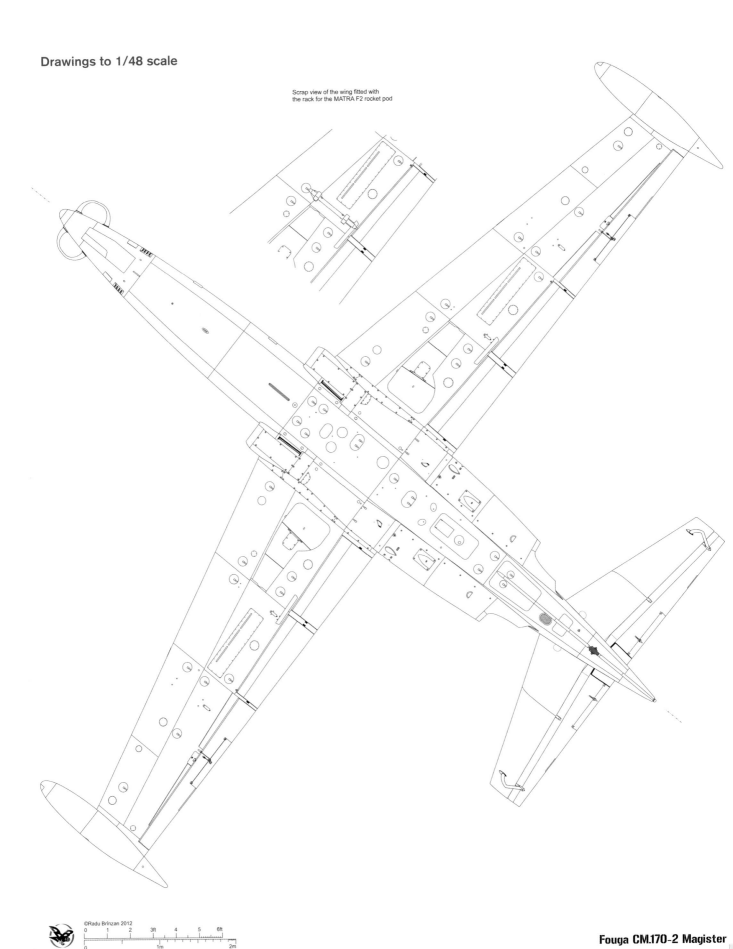

Fouga CM.170-2 Magister

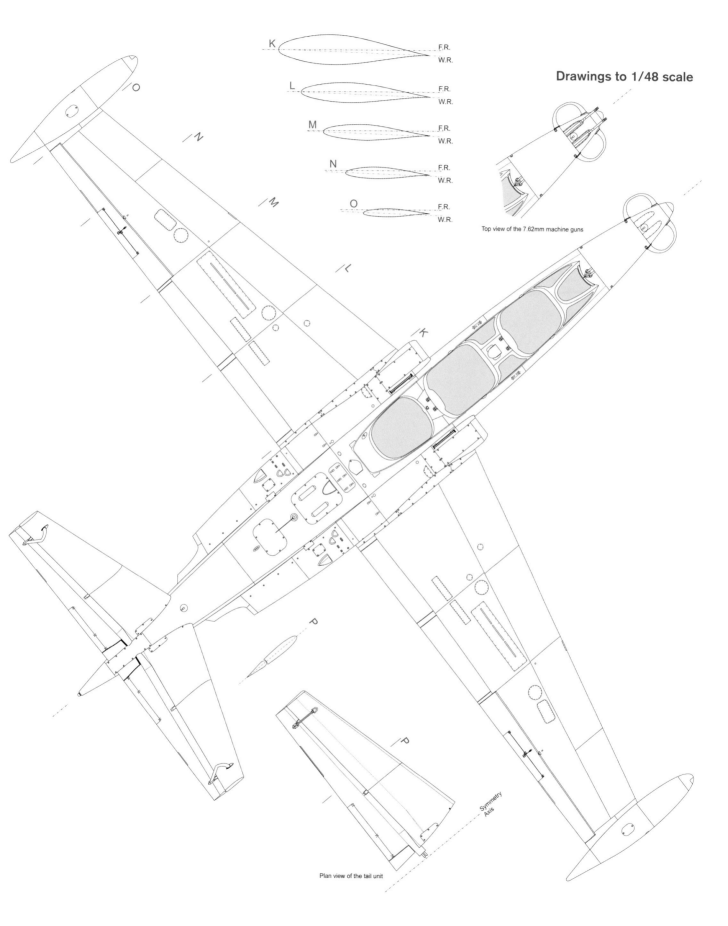

K — F.R.
— W.R.

L — F.R.
— W.R.

M — F.R.
— W.R.

N — F.R.
— W.R.

O — F.R.
— W.R.

Drawings to 1/48 scale

Top view of the 7.62mm machine guns

P

P

Symmetry
Axis

Plan view of the tail unit

0 1 2 3ft 4 5 6ft

0 1m 2m

Fouga CM.170-2 Magister

Three Fougas completing a formation loop near Baldonnel.
[Comdt. Dave Corcoran Photo]

Chapter 7

Wind-down and Replacement

After the Fougas were withdrawn from service, Fouga 215 was used as a Gate Guardian beside the passenger air terminal building at Baldonnel for a number of years before being transferrred to Dublin Institute of Technology, (Bolton Street) for use as an instructional airframe. [Lt. Col. Kevin Byrne Photo]

The Fouga Magister was an excellent advanced trainer for its day, but as time wore on, it was clear that this role could be carried out by more modern types at a lower cost. It wasn't just the cost of operating and maintaining a first-generation jet trainer that had been designed more than forty years previously that counted against keeping the Fouga in service. Their value as a training tool was also diminishing. As more modern operational types with 'glass' cockpits and digital displays came into service, the Fouga with its traditional analogue instruments and basic navigational aids was no longer a trainer that could prepare new pilots for the type of cockpit environment in which they would work. The Fouga had been replaced as a trainer by more sophisticated, higher performance aircraft in most countries that had operated the type and it was clear that a replacement would have to be found for the Fouga in Irish Air Corps service as well.

The Silver Swallows ceased operations as a display team in 1997, but the Fouga remained in Air Corps service for a further two years. The decision had been taken to retire the aircraft individually as they came due for a scheduled inspection. The first to be effectively withdrawn was Fouga 219 which last flew on 26 November 1996 and was used as a spares source for the remaining five aircraft during the 1997 display season. Fouga 215 was withdrawn in November 1997 with Fouga 216 performing its last flight on 16 December 1997. Fouga 217 and Fouga 218 carried out their last flights on 26 February 1998 and 20 April 1998 respectively. Fouga 220 was to continue flying up until June 1999 when it was last flown by Captain Justin Martin and Captain Christian Keegan.

There was never a formal stand down of Light Strike Squadron. As the number of aircraft gradually dwindled the personnel were re-assigned to other duties. Some of the pilots were posted to Maritime Squadron and the technical staff took over the maintenance of the then new Pilatus Britten-Norman BN-2T-4S Defender 4000 twin turboprop surveillance aircraft that was procured for the Garda (i.e., Irish Police) Air Support Unit in April 1997.

The Dassault/Dornier Alpha Jet was an advanced twin jet trainer that many in the Air Corps hoped would be the eventual replacement for the Fouga Magister. This French example was photographed at Florennes in Belgium in June 2012. [Peter Hopkins Photo]

As far back as 1986 when the Finnish Air Force had retired their Fouga Magisters, there had been speculation in Irish newspapers and within the Air Corps itself as to what types might ultimately replace the Fouga. Over the intervening years, Air Corps pilots had flown many of the potential Fouga replacements when given the opportunity to do so while on overseas visits to other air forces or when such aircraft visited Baldonnel. Individuals had their own favourites that they would have liked to have seen replacing the Fouga. Some would advocate the Dassault Alpha Jet as being the most logical replacement for the Fouga, as it was a twin engine aircraft like the Fouga but a much more high performance aircraft overall. Other Air Corps pilots had flown the BAe Hawk and were fans of that aircraft. No official requirement to replace the Fouga was ever issued while it was still in service. Unsolicited offers from a number of manufacturers did provide the Air Corps with the opportunity to fly a number of potential Fouga replacements but these flights were not formal evaluations per se. Nevertheless, test flights of various aircraft manufacturers products did ultimately inform the specification for the Fouga replacement. As Brigadier General Paul Fry recalls:

"I flew the Aermacchi MB339C in 1986, the developed MB326 which was a CM.170 competitor back in 1974 when we first looked at the Fouga. It had a similar limiting Mach number of 0.82 but its limiting indicated airspeed was 500knots, a full 100knots faster than the Fouga. The ejector seat – the first one I had ever flown upon, was very comfortable and the cockpit well-designed. It was fitted with an anti-g system and suit. It flew aerobatics very well, climbed like the proverbial home-sick angel and was

a tough, solid airframe capable of carrying twin 30mm pod-mounted cannon under the wings. The engine was responsive and powerful, with a single-push start button which was simplicity itself compared to the Fouga's levers and switches system. The engine was remarkably tolerant to use and abuse. This was demonstrated when I was allowed to fly a deliberate tail-slide, a manoeuvre which the Italian Air Force Major doing the aerobatics display had shown that morning during his practice and which all Air Corps personnel marvelled at, as it was thought that the Marborés wouldn't have taken kindly to such reverse airflows at all. The effect on the Fouga's butterfly tail was equally unknown but thought to have been capable of taking the flying surfaces off their hinges! The MB339 had an artificial horizon the size of a basketball which

The MB339 is the mount of the Frecce Tricolori Aerobatic Display Team. One of their aircraft is captured in this photo halfway through a tailslide, a manouevre that is not possible in many jet types! [Frank Grealish Photo]

was in direct contrast to the much smaller offering in the Fouga and gave a much clearer presentation.

I had flown the Pilatus PC7 Mk II (700shp) on 5 July 1995 when I was invited down from Gormanston by Commandant Jim Duffy, the OC BFTS/CFI, to take up a spare slot in a week-long evaluation of the type, courtesy of Pilatus. It was an impressive airplane and clearly a very real threat to the CM.170 jet replacement coming down the tracks, given the operating costs being so low. It could do the high altitude bit, added an ejector seat and had brand new avionics, etc. It was well-built and performed close to the CM.170 limits - or beyond in the case of pure g-forces where it had a working effective anti-g system to protect the pilot. It also had a stable-mate (the PC-9) with a 950shp powerplant too, offering even more performance.

I was also lucky enough to evaluate the Czech L-139 on 12 January 2000. The Defence White Paper hadn't been published then and the Air Corps still held out hope for a jet-powered replacement for the Fouga. The L-139 was a development of the successful East European Aero L-39 trainer type, with a Garrett TFE731-4 engine and plans for western avionics. Its flight envelope was the same as the CM.170, redlined indicated air speed at 400knots and Mach 0.82, with a bit more g tolerance if I recall (+6g to -3g) and thankfully an anti-g suit and also a Flight Visions FV4000 Head Up Display (HUD). The endurance had been increased by 45 minutes due to the lower fuel consumption of the western engine, giving it around three hours endurance in total. It had some interesting student-proofing features such as the flaps that would automatically retract if you reached the limiting speed and the airbrake would deploy if you reached the Vne or Mach number. If you decided to ignore them and

'shove the nose forward' the airbrakes came out further - they were full span under the wing, the airbrakes bridging the gap between the ailerons. It was thus impossible to exceed any of the speed limits, and yes, we all tried! On the HUD there also was an air-to-air training mode which allowed the instructor to bring up a target aircraft on the front seat HUD and 'fly' it around the screen while the student attempted to get a 'guns' sight picture on it. The whole thing was recorded for de-briefing and proved how useful a training aid it could be. Ultimately this experience informed the case for a HUD in the PC-9M".

The Defence White Paper referred to above was published in February 2000 and set out the Irish Government's medium term strategy for defence covering the period up to 2010, based on the evolving national and international security environment at the time. The White Paper outlined the defence strategy for the Army, Navy and Air Corps. Notwithstanding some lobbying from Air Corps personnel prior to its publication, it was stated in the White Paper that:

'The generally favourable security climate resulted in the need for a very limited military air capability. To exceed this capability would require a level of investment in personnel, equipment and infrastructure which could not be justified.'

The White Paper referred to the pragmatic approach taken by the Air Corps in providing a limited clear-weather ground attack/support capability and airspace control limited to low level and favourable visibility using the aircraft with which they were equipped, but there was no requirement to exceed this limited capability with any new aircraft type purchased.

The Aermacchi MB339 was another aircraft that would have been suitable as a Fouga Magister replacement. This example attended the 'Air Spectacular' at Baldonnel in 1986, where Air Corps pilots were given the opportunity to fly it.
[Christopher Roche Photo]

Right: The Aero L-139 Albatros was also marketed as a replacement for the Fouga. Equipped with western avionics and engine, the type was test flown by Air Corps pilots in January 2000.
[Air Corps Photo Section]

In response to those who had advocated a limited air defence capability, the Defence White Paper went on to state that:

'Aspirations to broaden the range of available air based capabilities are understandable but have to be balanced against real world constraints. The fact is that, given the enormous costs involved, few small countries possess the ability to provide a comprehensive air based defence capability. The choice must then lie between maintaining an essentially token force to address all dimensions of national defence or seeking to perform a selected range of tasks to a professional standard. The latter option has been the one chosen in Ireland.'

With regard to replacing the Marchetti and Cessna 172 (no mention was made of the Fouga as it had already been withdrawn from use) it was stated that:

'The cost of acquiring, maintaining and operating even a small number of such aircraft will be an important consideration. As always, such costs have to be viewed in terms of their opportunity cost elsewhere in denying resources to other defence equipment.'

With such a strong emphasis on costs, this effectively ruled out any jet powered replacement for the Fouga, but the White paper did set out a plan for the next ten years and made it clear that funding was available at last to begin the process of fleet replacement. The Air Corps assembled a team to draw up the specification for whatever new aircraft would replace the Marchetti/Fouga combination that had served the Air Corps so well for over twenty years.

As Brigadier General Fry recalls:

"The challenge from the outset was to purchase a trainer that could do operational tasks and low-level air defence and flying training from 'ab initio' stage upwards. The type had to be a jet or have nearly the performance

of a jet type, so a turboprop trainer (as opposed to a piston-engine type) was pretty much the choice from the word go. As an aside, the Czechs had told us they had tried an experiment training pilots on L-39 jet type straight through their 'Wings' course comparing the results to phasing them through on light piston, medium piston and then jet. They said yes, it worked, gave a high quality graduate but was a very expensive course and they wouldn't recommend it as the additional cost of failures - cadets who did not pass at the solo-stage or later - was exorbitant and drove the overall cost/benefit figures out of sight".

Some of the requirements for the aircraft that would enable the Air Corps to implement the new syllabus included the following features:

- A turboprop engine for high power output (750 shp to 1650 shp) enabling use of medium or high altitudes up to 30,000 feet.
- The aircraft would have to have a high dive speed and Mach number together with a high cruise speed, as close as possible to that of the Fouga Magister jet.
- It should be capable of being armed with a variety of guns and rockets.
- It should also have weapons sighting systems including air-to-air predicting facility restoring the ability to train in this role.
- The turboprop was also required to be very fuel efficient, giving internal fuel endurance of 3.5 hours which exceeds that of the Marchetti by one hour and in the case of the Magister, by two hours.
- Safety features, such as the inclusion of ejector seats, were also specified.
- The range of the aircraft should be capable of being extended via under wing fuel tanks.
- Maintenance should be made easier by the use of modular systems.

When the tender for the Fouga/Marchetti replacement was finally published in 2002 the Embraer Super Tucano was one of the types evaluated. [Ricardo Hebmuller photo]

The Department of Defence published the tender documentation for the new trainer in 2002 and shortly thereafter the Air Corps shortlisted three types for full evaluation, the Swiss built Pilatus PC-9 powered by a 900 hp engine, the Brazilian Embraer Super Tucano with a 1650 hp engine and the American Raytheon T-6A Texan II powered by a 1250 hp engine. All three were very good aircraft. The PC-9 had an excellent track record of sales to major air arms throughout the world. The Super Tucano had been derived from its predecessor the Embraer Tucano which had achieved sales of over 700 aircraft and was designed for border patrol and counter insurgency roles in addition to its advanced training role. The Raytheon T-6 Texan II was itself derived from the Pilatus PC-9 but substantially redesigned to meet the specifications of the JPATS competition in the US to provide a trainer for the US Air Force and US Navy. After a thorough evaluation the Pilatus PC-9M was chosen as the winner and eight of these aircraft were purchased, the first three being delivered on 21 April 2004.

As Brigadier General Fry describes it:

"In the event, the PC-9M won the competition and we've had a good working relationship with the aircraft and its manufacturers from the word go. We devised

a new training syllabus in collaboration with Pilatus, taking into account their other customers' experiences with the type and the company's own expertise in designing such programmes. The new training syllabus as originally devised consisted of three distinct phases. The Elementary Flying Training (EFT) phase would include instruction on basic turns, climbs, descent, stalling, aerobatics, takeoff and landing. The Basic Flying Training (BFT) phase would expand upon the basic skills and introduce the student pilot to day and night navigation, instrument flying and formation flying. The Advanced Flying Training (AFT) phase would further expand the skills of the student pilot by exploring the high altitude and high speed corners of the envelope. It was a good experience for us and the syllabus has evolved in the years since the PC-9M was introduced to service, getting the most from its performance. The revised syllabus doesn't seek to separate the air exercises and progression of the traditional EFT, BFT and AFT phases which had previously characterised the skills and training progressions of the old aircraft types (Chipmunk, Provost and Vampire and later Marchetti and Fouga Magister).

High altitude flight, above 10,000 feet and previously the domain of the former jet types - is now used routinely during EFT and BFT training. The PC-9M can thus exploit the good flying conditions at high altitude, making the best use of the weather and airspace available even on EFT exercises. The AFT skills now centre around high performance, operational and tactical type exercises such as high-speed, low-level navigation, airways and procedural flying and formation leading skillsets.

It's giving us a very high quality product (trained pilots) which can handle the demands of our operational types, which is what its primary function is and it's doing the armed tasks very well also. The training task has been eased by the addition of a simulator, with time spent in the simulator prior to flight training being of enormous benefit to the training progression when you

Members of the team that evaluated the Super Tucano from L-R Lieutenant Colonel Paul Fry, Commandant Rory O'Connor and Lieutenant Paul Kelly. [Brig. Gen. Paul Fry Collection]

Above: The second aircraft to be evaluated was the Raytheon T-6 Texan II, a type derived from the Pilatus PC-9 but built to satisfy USAF requirements. The example shown here is a Greek Air Force machine. [Will Dempsey Photo]

Below: The Pilatus PC-9 was the third aircraft to be evaluated as a potential Fouga/Marchetti replacement. From the Left: Comdt Rory O'Connor, OC FTS; Lt Paul Kelly, QFI FTS; Mr Jimmy Sewell, Contracts Officer, Department of Defence; Lt Col P Fry, President of Fixed-Wing Trainer Evaluation Board; Capt Colin Roche , Engineer Officer FTS; Flight Sgt Brendan "Flint" Higgins (RIP), Flight Sergeant FTS [Brig. Gen. Paul Fry Collection]

get the Cadets into the air. The addition of the HUD was a foothold into the technology of fighters which was intended to keep us at the races in this area. The FV4000 Head Up Display offered a significant step forward for us in terms of technology and flight experience, and added a modern aspect to our weapons aiming and delivery skills. It also has a potent air-to-air mode which is capable of giving accuracy levels way beyond those of the gyro-stabilised sighting system of the Vampire (the Fouga only having a simple fixed gunsight). The 12.7mm guns and 2.75" rockets are also a step beyond the 7.62mm and 68mm SNEBs of the Fouga and Marchetti".

Fouga Magisters – Out of Service but still useful

With the final flight of a Fouga in Irish Air Corps service taking place in June 1999, the issue was what to do with the airframes. There was really no question of selling them on to another air force as

their efficacy as a trainer was at an end for the reasons described above. However, they still had potential use as ground instructional airframes. In the event three of the Fougas were to continue in use for this role. Paul Gibbons had worked on the aircraft in Baldonnel but had left to work as a lecturer in aircraft systems at Carlow Institute of Technology. An approach was made to the Air Corps to ascertain if they would be willing to part with one of their retired Fougas as Paul felt it would be ideal for demonstrating aircraft systems and structures to students at Carlow IT. The Air Corps agreed and Fouga 220 was delivered to Carlow IT in April 2001. Following a period in storage the aircraft was re-assembled in a purpose built training hangar at Carlow IT where it continues to be a valuable training aid to student aircraft engineers.

Similarly, Fouga 218 was presented to the FÁS Shannon Training Centre in Co. Clare in July 2002 and Fouga 215 was delivered to the Dublin Institute of Technology (Bolton Street) in November 2004 for use as instructional airframes by student engineers in these establishments.

A similar use was proposed for Fouga 216 at a training college in Cork and it was moved down to Cork Airport. It languished there for a number of years stored out in the open. Sergeant Pat Cornally had fond memories of Fouga 216 as it was the first aircraft for which he was NCO in charge. As Pat recalls:

"When I was given charge of 216 I didn't even own a car so I had a soft spot for that particular aircraft much as most drivers remember the first car they ever owned. I was sorry to see it leave Baldonnel for Cork in 2002. A few years later I travelled down to Cork as part of the crew on a Casa maritime patrol aircraft and I was

shocked to see the state of 216. The Irish weather had really taken its toll on the aircraft and it was in a sorry state. Fortunately the powers that be felt moved to bring 216 back to Baldonnel. Over a period of years it was fully restored to display condition".

Fouga 216 and its counterpart Fouga 219 which had been retained by the Air Corps are both on display at the Air Corps Museum and Heritage Centre at Baldonnel. What remains of 221, the instructional airframe coded 3-KE is also stored at Baldonnel in a dismantled state.

Going Full Circle –
Fouga 217 Goes Back to Austria.

The Austrian Air Force maintains an excellent museum at Zeltweg containing examples of most, if not all, types operated by that air arm since 1955. One notable omission until 2005 was that of a Fouga Magister. As recounted in Chapter 3, the Austrian Air Force operated no less than 18 of this type from 1959 until 1972 but no example remained in Austria, as the surviving examples were sold back to the manufacturer in part exchange for helicopters. When the Austrians

became aware that the Air Corps had retired the Fouga, and given the fact the no less than four of the six had been ex-Austrian Air Force machines, the Austrians were keen to obtain one of them for display in the museum at Zeltweg.

The then General Officer Commanding the Air Corps, Brigadier General (currently Major General and Deputy Chief of Staff of the Defence Forces) Ralph James was delighted to assist the Austrian Air Force with their request. Fouga 217 was one of the original Austrian Fouga Magisters and this aircraft was selected for return to Austria. Project manager for the task was Commandant John Sweeney of No 4 Support Wing who also acted as liaison officer to the Austrians. For their part, the latter were acting through First Lieutenant Silvan Fuegenschuh, who was familiar with the special requirements of carrying a dismantled jet inside a transport aircraft.

The Austrian Air Force operates three ex-RAF Lockheed C-130 Hercules transport aircraft and two of these were used to transport Fouga 217 back to Austria. Because specialist loading equipment was available at Dublin Airport, Fouga 217 was dismantled and separated into two loads

After a thorough evaluation the aircraft chosen to replace the Fouga/ Marchetti combination was the Pilatus PC-9M.
In this photo two Irish Air Corps PC-9Ms are seen in the company of Irish Naval vessel L. E. Eithne.
[Air Corps Photo Section]

Fouga 217, now wearing its
original Austrian markings
of 4D-YL on display in the
Austrian Air Force Museum
at Zeltweg.
[J. Maxwell photo]

for transport there by road before commencing the onward journey to Zeltweg. The fuselage was taken there on 30 March 2005 on board Hercules 8T-CC with the wings and other components returning the next day on board Hercules 8T-CA. Within a short time Fouga 217 was repainted in full Austrian markings and wearing its original Austrian Air Force serial of 4D-YL. It is currently on display to the public at the museum at Zeltweg.

The Fouga Magister flew with no less than twenty air arms throughout the world and was without doubt one of the most successful jet trainers of all time. It was in service in one form or another for over forty years and several are still flying in civilian hands. It was used in the armed role on several occasions in conflicts in the Middle East, Africa and South America. As a replacement for the De Havilland Vampire T.55

it was a good choice for the Irish Air Corps too. The Fouga has gone from Irish Air Corps service for over a decade but it's still fondly remembered by those that flew and maintained it as a very fine aircraft. No less than 113 pilots obtained their "wings" during the 24 years it was in service and many others became instructors on the type. It became famous in Ireland as the mount for the Silver Swallows Aerobatic Display Team and they reached the pinnacle of international achievement by being awarded the Lockheed Martin Cannestra Trophy for the best display by an overseas display team at the Royal International Air Tattoo in 1997. Military flying is a hazardous profession at the best of times. The fact that no one was killed or seriously injured while flying the Fouga in Irish Air Corps service is reason alone for it having a special place in the memory of those who flew and maintained it in Ireland.

Fouga 217 was transported
in two separate loads,
fuselage in one and wings
and other components in
the second load.
[Photo courtesy of the
Austrian Air Force]